Haute
JEWELRY

BY CAROLINE CHILDERS

BW PUBLISHING ASSOCIATES, INC.
In Association with
Rizzoli International Publications, Inc.

FIRST PUBLISHED IN THE UNITED STATES OF AMERICA IN 1999 BY

Ms. Caroline Childers and
BW Publishing Associates, Inc.
11 West 25th Street, New York, NY 10010

In association with Rizzoli International Publications, Inc.
300 Park Avenue South, New York, NY 10010

ISBN: 0-8478-2190-0

LIBRARY OF CONGRESS CATALOG CARD NUMBER: 98-68532

CHAIRMAN
Joseph Zerbib

CHIEF EXECUTIVE OFFICER AND PUBLISHER
Caroline Childers

PRESIDENT
Yael Choukroun

LOGO BY DANIELLE LOUFRANI

PRINTED IN HONG KONG

COVER
Chopard's "Haute Joaillerie" collection necklace in 18K white gold set with 502 square-cut and trapeze-cut diamonds totaling 126.98 carats and seven rubies totaling 45.58 carats.

INSIDE FRONT FLAP
Earrings set with diamonds, rubies and emerald drops, by de Grisogono.

BACK COVER
"Ice Cube" watch on a satin bracelet designed by de Grisogono for Chopard.

INSIDE BACK FLAP
Brooch in diamonds and invisibly set rubies by Verdura.

OPENING PAGE
Brooch composed of a carved jade panel inserted between two semicircles that are pavé set with brilliant diamonds and framed by two carved, fan-shaped motifs made of rock crystal. Mounted in platinum and gray gold. Boucheron, 1934.

ABOVE
Diana cameo in sardonyx shell mounted in an interwoven frame in 18K gold with diamonds by Roberta.

BELOW LEFT
Bracelets in 18K gold from Carrera y Carrera.

FACING PAGE
Piranesi Haute Joaillerie necklace in diamonds set in platinum with a 60-carat emerald pendant. Diamond earrings set in platinum with two emerald pendants totaling 80 carats.

Contents

Haute Jewelry

Houses of Prestige

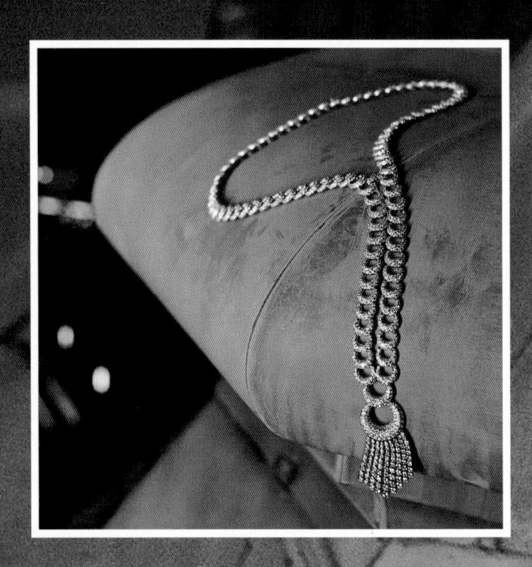

LEFT
Haute Jewelry by Chaumet

FACING PAGE
Martin Gruber's one-of-a-kind jewelry created exclusively for HAUTE JEWELRY.

Foreword

There was a time when only royalty could experience the unmatched splendor of haute jewelry. Today, jewelry designs have been transformed — altering to keep pace with the changing styles of the modern world even as they maïntain a classic spirit of beauty and elegance. An exceptional designer can make a women feel like a queen, simply by creating items that reflect her personal beauty. It may take but one diamond or ruby surrounded in gold to present the true radiance of a woman.

As technology and communication have narrowed the boundaries between cultures, there has been a rise in the availability and appeal of exotic styles. Jewelers such as Boucheron have found inspiration in the ancient treasures found in the tombs of Egypt's pharaohs. Caroline Gruosi-Scheufele drew inspiration from the Far East to create the Casmir collection for Chopard. Piranesi has recreated popular designs from European royalty that are currently enjoying a renaissance. And Ilias Lalaounis transforms the circuitry of computers into extraordinary jewels.

FACING PAGE
Haute Joaillerie by Piranesi. Necklace with rubies totaling 300 carats and diamonds totaling 150 carats set in platinum. Earrings with rubies totaling 30 carats and diamonds totaling 20 carats set in platinum.

BELOW
Bracelet with rubies totaling 48 carats and diamonds totaling 25 carats set in platinum.

While this book concentrates on the great jewelers of Europe and North America, it also reflects the global influences that have broadened the scope of jewelry design over its long history. Surveying the history of haute jewelry takes us on a fascinating journey, reflecting both the passage of time and the extraordinary diversity of cultures and designs from around the world.

Many of the jewelers in this book who are well known to the public were once the exclusive designers to kings and queens. As these brilliant designers have broadened their mission and their reach, jewelry designs have been transformed — altering to keep pace with the changing styles of the modern world even as they maintain a classic spirit of beauty and elegance.

Fine jewelry can be exceptionally valuable and collectible, but it is not made for the bank vault — the pieces seen in this book are meant to be worn and appreciated in all of their spectacular glory.

Caroline Childers

Acknowledgements

We want to express our sincerest gratitude and appreciation to the many people who offered their knowledge and tireless assistance to this project: Mr. Alexandre Reza, Paris; Mr. Alain Boucheron, Mr. Jean-Claude Le Rouzic, Ms. Murielle Blanchard, Ms. Claudine Sablier from Boucheron, Paris; Mr. Gerard Pichon-Varin from Boucheron, New York; Ms. Jackie Pinto, Mr. Gordon Roberts, Ms. Christina Murphy, Ms. Sheila White from Chanel, New York; Ms.Valerie Dupont, Ms. Melanie Joire, Mr. Jean-Claude Barde from Chanel, Paris; Ms. Evelyne Menager, Mr. Pierre Haquet from Chaumet, Paris; Mr. Daniel Bogue from Chaumet, New York; Ms. Caroline Gruosi-Scheufele and Ms. Annick Benoit-Godet from Chopard, Genève; Mr. Roberto Coin, Ms. Pilar Coin, Ms. Alessandra Lavinato from Roberto Coin, Vincenza; Mr. Fawaz Gruosi, Ms. Michele Reichenbach from de Grisogono, Genève; Mr. Martin Gruber, Mr. David Michael Evans from Nova Styling, Van Nuys, California; Ms. Angelique Lalaounis, Mr. Ilias Lalaounis from Lalaounis, Athens; Ms. Dimitra Lalaounis from Lalaounis, London; Eli Antoniades from Lalaounis, New York; Ms. Doris Panos, Ms. Mona Taner, Mr. Chris Nasisoglu, Ms. Melissa Kulhanjian from Doris Panos, New York; Ms. Maria Carla Picchiotti from Picchiotti, Valenza; Mr. Samy Piranesi, Mr. Michel Piranesi from Piranesi, New York; Mr. Jack Piranesi from Piranesi, Milano; Mrs. Roberta Apa-Colombo from Roberta, Milano; Ms. Marie Moatti-Beauchard from Van Cleef & Arpels, Paris; Mr.Edward Landrigan, Mr. Robert Dwy, Mr. Michael Jacque from Verdura, New York; Mr. Giovanni Mattera, Ms. Eleanor Kihlberg from Gianni Versace, New York; Ms. Andrea Trimolado, Ms. Margherita Caccavale from Gianni Versace, Milano.

This book required the careful attention of all those involved in its production: Natalie Warady, Ted Davis, Lynn Braz, Caroline Elbaz-Ruiz, Danielle Loufrani, Dan Geist, Dayne Kelly and Angela Van Amburg for publishing this book. Jack Silberstein and Deborah Darseyne for their photographic expertise. Ms. Solveig Williams, Mr. John Brancati, Mr. Antonio Polito and Ms. Katherine Adzima of Rizzoli International Publications who guided us through each phase of production. To my lawyer Marianne Gaertner Dorado. And to Frenchway Travel, who make the impossible, possible... with passion.

CAROLINE CHILDERS

Our most heartfelt thanks is extended to Joseph Zerbib,
a tireless source of strength who supported us every step of the way and
without whom HAUTE JEWELRY *would not have been possible.*

THIS PAGE
Haute Joaillerie by Alexandre Reza. Necklace with a fancy intense yellow diamond weighing more than 10 carats with an oval emerald weighing 7 carats. Matching ring with emerald and diamonds.

Introduction

TURNING FANTASY INTO REALITY

Having been raised in a family of jewelers, there is a great heritage of gems in my bloodline — you might say I have high jewelry in my genes. Certainly, the creation of such jewels is a passion that encompasses my life. I work with stones millions of years old, a fact that makes my task both humbling and inspiring. Nothing can surpass the enchantment of a perfect, precious gemstone. The effect such a stone has on its beholder is similar to that of a painting by one of the great masters; as one gazes into the depths of a gem one can always see a more compelling beauty within.

My favorite of all gems is the sapphire. I adore the essence of the color blue, a color steeped in mythology. Considered a bridge to the heavens when the world was believed to be flat, it was thought that the only way to reach the gods was through the blue sky. One fable tells of a princess who spent endless days waiting for her prince to return. Finally, believing that he was never coming back, she threw herself into a lake and drowned. On that same day, the prince returned, expectant for his true love, but finding only her two blue eyes transformed into a pair of sapphires adrift in the water.

FACING PAGE
Fancy, intense yellow diamond set in yellow gold between two diamonds mounted in platinum. Boucheron.

At Boucheron, we turn fantasy into reality, translating images like the sapphire legend into beautiful jewels. We continually strive to compose designs that create a classic harmony, a symphony of shape and color, form and fashion. The finest representation of this harmony is a captivating, seductive woman herself. Flattering the natural beauty of such a woman, Boucheron's jewelry cambers and arches in symmetry with the graceful, alluring curves that define femininity. One never tires of such a piece of jewelry — it shimmers constantly, capturing the eye, and the soul.

As Chairman of the Board, it is my job to make sure everything that comes out of our ateliers is worthy of the Boucheron name. I examine every gem and approve each design. Twelve years ago, Boucheron was a name treasured by the select few, but unknown or thought unattainable by the general public. My desire was to broaden the reach and appeal of our jewelry, to make it accessible to more people, and of course, ensure that the Boucheron name and product meet in ultimate beauty to be cherished by women for generations to come.

ALAIN BOUCHERON

Introduction

Reinventing Glamor

Belonging to the rich past of Chopard has enabled me to fill the future with a world of sparkling jewels. I embellish the traditions I have learned with the creativity that comes from within, always striving to keep a continual advancement in the company's designs. While remaining adherent to themes I have developed, I work to enhance and expand them. For instance, I am proud of each new addition to the "Happy Diamonds" jewelry line, Chopard's most successful collection, particularly the "Happy Sport" line, which I think best echoes the spirit of modern women.

Chopard is continually expanding its horizons, not only by opening exclusive Chopard boutiques in numerous cities around the world, but by becoming involved in such prestigious events as the Cannes International Film Festival. In doing so, Chopard is linking its history with one of the film world's greatest and most glamorous occasions — I

enjoyed the honor of redesigning the festival's top award, the Palme d'Or, which is now etched with Chopard's name. The sponsorship has presented many thrills for me as a jewelry designer. It was certainly a joy to see our haute joaillerie worn by famous actresses and models, and to witness a traditional company that is more than 100 years old revel in the glamor that it deserves.

I have often said that it is my personal joy to create jewelry that makes women feel beautiful. The Casmir collection, a mixture of the Orient and the Western world, is a particular favorite of mine. The unique combination of arabesques and floral patterns have opened a new world of jewelry to us. My next endeavor is the Pushkin collection, reflecting the spirit of the Russian people, another exotic beauty I dreamt of exploring. There is no end to the inspiration capable of fulfilling the ongoing collections worthy of the Chopard legacy, a tradition I am proud to be a part of.

CAROLINE GRUOSI-SCHEUFELE

FACING PAGE
Jewelry set in 18K white gold. Necklace flowers set with diamonds and heart-shaped sapphires. Earclips set with diamonds and heart-shaped sapphires.

Introduction

Discovering a Legacy of Design

Fulco di Verdura's sense of style — witty, fanciful and classical — is brought to life in jewelry designs that forever place Verdura in exclusive company. While Verdura is one of the most imitated jewelers of this century, his name is still unknown by the general public. The select appeal of Verdura is no accident, as each piece is custom fit and limited in its production. Today, we are diligent in our efforts to ensure that the Verdura name remains an ideal, as we draw from the legacy of designs that he produced. His wonderful use of color and form established a distinctive style that to this day possesses a special power to enchant.

With the recent opening of Verdura's second boutique in Palm Beach, Florida, we hope to introduce new generations to the magic of Verdura. We will continue our intimate, decades-old salon approach in this new boutique, ensuring that we do not lose our unique identity. We will also continue to uphold Verdura's devotion to truly original and lasting style, which rises above that of passing trends. In this way, we will maintain the enduring spirit of Verdura into the next century.

Ward Landrigan

FACING PAGE
Diamond brooch by Verdura.

Introduction

A Love Affair with Diamonds

Inspired by our love for all things beautiful, Gianni and I decided in the late 1980s to create exclusive pieces of fine jewelry. The first collection featured exquisite diamonds in combination with rubies and yellow gold or sapphires and white gold — resulting in jewelry with an intense, unique dynamism.

The Versace collection continues today to be striking and daring — perfectly suited to evening wear or a simple pair of jeans — and it is created specially for those who love to be admired and do not fear boldness.

At the heart of the Versace collection is my lifelong love for diamonds, and as the line of jewelry has developed and grown, so too has my fascination and admiration for these precious stones. I take great care with each individual design and I personally ensure that the jewelry's standards always honor the Versace image. I am confident that Versace jewelry will become synonymous with the perfection of diamonds just as Versace clothing has become an undeniable part of fashion history.

Donatella Versace

FACING PAGE
Four d-flawless diamond rings by Versace.

Introduction

Capturing the Essence of Gems

FACING PAGE
Parure of rubies, necklace, ring and earrings. Alexandre Reza.

Having traveled the entire world in relentless pursuit of nature's most exquisite stones, I have grown to understand the patience and grace that is necessary when creating works of art that look nothing short of priceless. Stones that have existed for hundreds of thousands of years — once unearthed — must find a new place where they may sparkle at the zenith of their brilliance. Once the right setting is unveiled, perfection is achieved and the moment is magical. Guided by an unfailing instinct and masterful skill, I am continually pursuing my goal of bringing this magic and sophistication back to fine jewelry while also reinventing new beauty that will forever burn brightly for the woman of today.

Alexandre Reza

Tiaras

Crowning Celebration of Jewelry

Cleopatra's was serpentine, in honor of Isis. Diana's was diamond laden but mostly safe-deposit box hidden. Charles, when inaugurated Prince of Wales, opted for a table-tennis ball spray-painted gold. Henry the Eighth favored velvet, Napoleon fancied bees and King Tut, during his youthful reign, was partial to vultures. And consciously or not, each of them wore their symbols of royalty, power, wealth and divinity where the message would be most conspicuous — atop their illustrious heads. At the summit of every aristocrat rests a piece of jewelry that stakes its sovereignty: A tiara, a diadem, a crown.

ABOVE
Magnificent diamond and emerald tiara by Alexandre Reza.

FACING PAGE
Cleopatra. Oil painting by Gustave Moreau. The Louvre, Paris.

Self-adornment, it would seem, is as natural to man — and, of course, woman — as eating and sleeping. By 30,000 BC, hunters were wearing animal bones, most likely as talismans for successful hunting as well as ornamentation. In fact, the roles of adornments and amulets are inextricably interwoven. For jewelry, one of the oldest genres of decorative art, symbolism is intrinsic. And symbolically, a decorated head is nothing short of royal.

RIGHT
Flute player wears tiara in gold leaf. 5th century.

FAR RIGHT
Design for ruby and diamond tiara, which could also be worn on the shoulder. 1937. Chaumet.

CENTER RIGHT
Mural painting, The Recognition of Hercules by Telephe. Naples Museum.

BELOW
167K gold ciboriom decorated with lapis lazuli, 1935. Boucheron collection.

BOTTOM RIGHT
Athena Parthenos with serpent and shield. Antique copy in marble of the Parthenon statue by Phidias, 5th century BC, National Archaeological Museum, Athens.

Hair ornaments, dating from 2500 BC, were discovered in the royal tomb of Babylonian Queen Pu-abi. Her complex headdress was made from strings of tubular beads, gold and lapis lazuli discs and garlands of gold leaves, with a lattice of gold ribbons surmounted by a tall crest of three golden flowers. The extravagant funerary customs of ancient courts ordered the entombment of servants, guards and musicians along with the deceased royalty: thus, among the sixty-three members of Pu-abi's tomb entourage, are women who wear more modest versions — simple golden leaves — of the Queen's headbands.

In Egypt, where the art of creating jewelry flourished as early as 4000 BC, an extensive variety of diadems and head ornaments are prominently featured in wall paintings and sculptures. Delicate circlets of gold wires set with flowers fashioned from colored stones — most likely in imitation of fresh-cut flowers that were spun into hair accents — were worn by Princess Khnumet at Dahshur around 1895 BC. Also, young princesses of that time shaved their heads and donned jeweled wigs, such as those worn by Princess Sit-Hathor-Yunet in 1850 BC. Her thick hair was divided

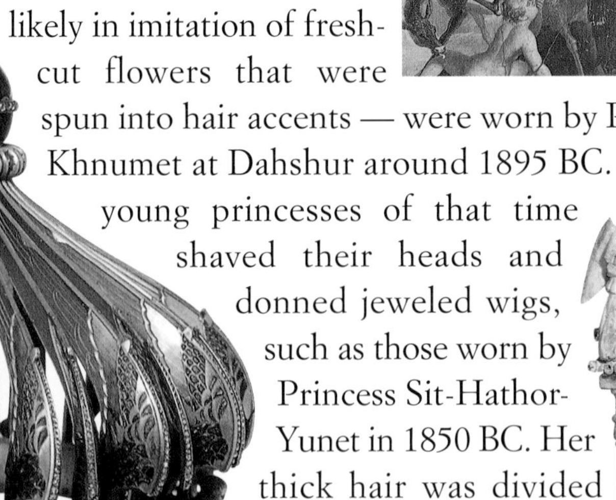

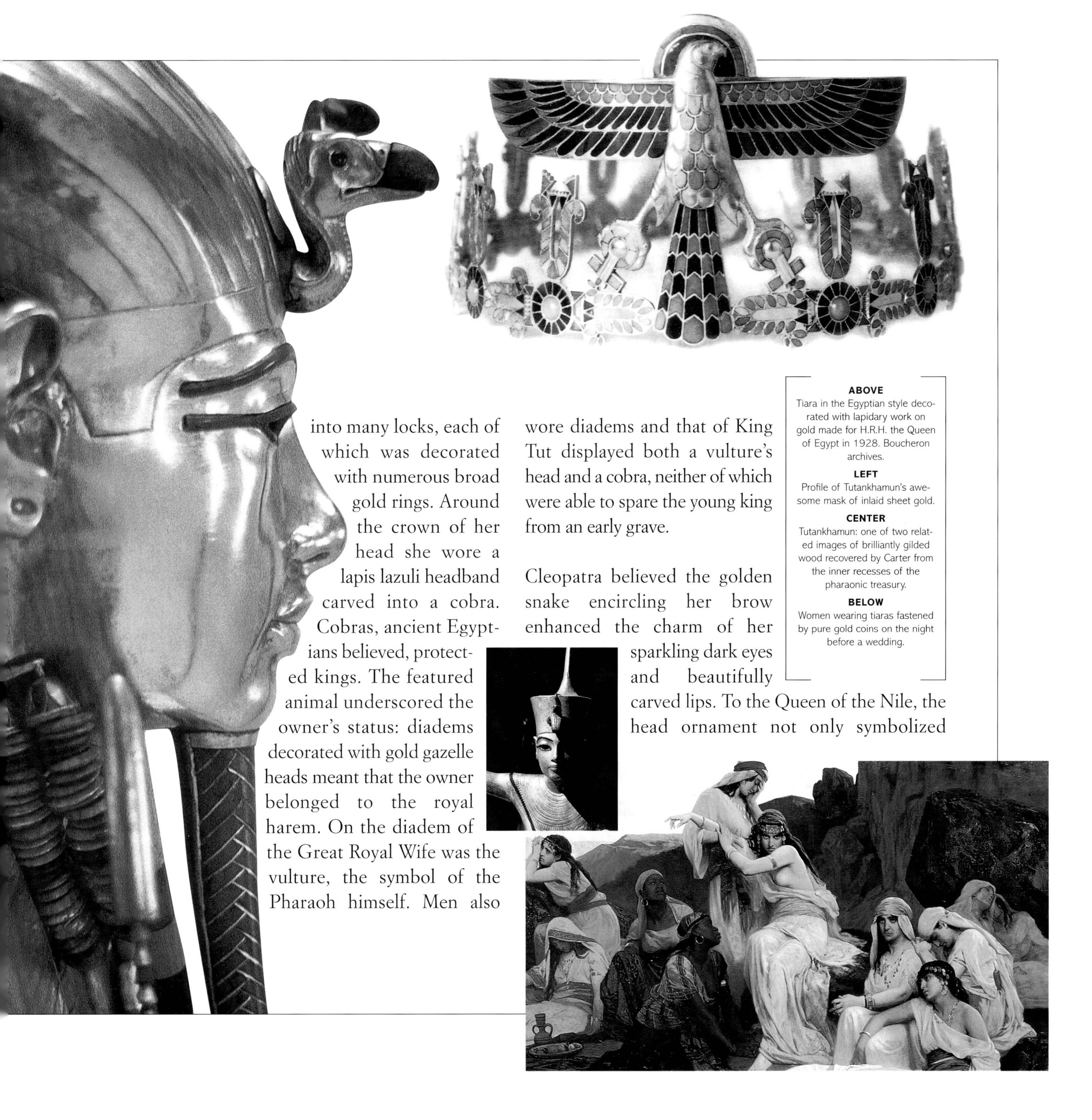

into many locks, each of which was decorated with numerous broad gold rings. Around the crown of her head she wore a lapis lazuli headband carved into a cobra. Cobras, ancient Egyptians believed, protected kings. The featured animal underscored the owner's status: diadems decorated with gold gazelle heads meant that the owner belonged to the royal harem. On the diadem of the Great Royal Wife was the vulture, the symbol of the Pharaoh himself. Men also wore diadems and that of King Tut displayed both a vulture's head and a cobra, neither of which were able to spare the young king from an early grave.

Cleopatra believed the golden snake encircling her brow enhanced the charm of her sparkling dark eyes and beautifully carved lips. To the Queen of the Nile, the head ornament not only symbolized

ABOVE
Tiara in the Egyptian style decorated with lapidary work on gold made for H.R.H. the Queen of Egypt in 1928. Boucheron archives.

LEFT
Profile of Tutankhamun's awesome mask of inlaid sheet gold.

CENTER
Tutankhamun: one of two related images of brilliantly gilded wood recovered by Carter from the inner recesses of the pharaonic treasury.

BELOW
Women wearing tiaras fastened by pure gold coins on the night before a wedding.

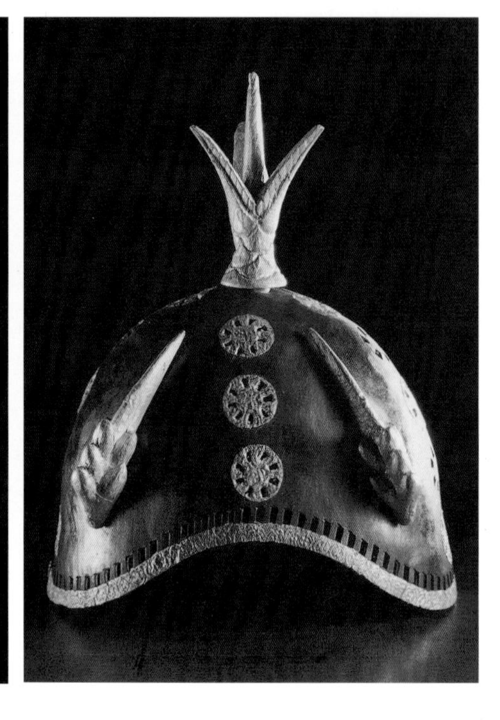

power, but actually bestowed it as well. About her favorite goddess, Isis, after whom she fashioned herself, Cleopatra declared, "Sunlight flashed from the feathers of her gold hawk wings, from the ruby eyes of her uraeus." And in her later years, according to historian Reverend Ruth G. Svendsen, Cleopatra "often wore a gold mesh cap closely studded with little matched pearls to which were attached here and there, sometimes dangling as pendants, rubies, emeralds, sapphires and diamonds of different shapes. They represented the stars." Marc Antony, says Svendsen, wore a masculine version of the same piece, representing the sun: "From a little gold disc on the back of his head a few long fragile gold spikes projected downward on which were sparingly and artfully attached tiny gems." Ancient civilization's most notorious couple were thus identified with the celestial — and the divine.

TOP LEFT
Atilla the Hun, wearing a gold tiara with precious stones.

TOP CENTER
Tiara of Queen Constance of Aragon, 12th century.

TOP RIGHT
Tiara made with skin of antelope covered with gold leaf. 19th century Ghana.

CENTER
Tiara made in pure gold from the islands of Nias.

The Greeks brought new gemstones, designs and techniques to jewelry. Clusters of colored

RIGHT
Princess from the Ivory Coast on her engagement day.
LEFT
Princess of Siam wearing a parure and tiara of gold, diamonds, pearls and rubies.
FAR RIGHT
Queen of Bulgaria wearing a tiara by Boucheron.

RIGHT
Princess Diana of Wales wearing a tiara of diamonds and pearls.
CENTER
Tiara from Nepal during the 15th Century, made in gilt bronze and precious stones.
FAR RIGHT
Rising Sun Aigrette Chaumet

FAR LEFT
Princess of Sudan, Africa on the day of her wedding.
CENTER
Helen of Troy's diadem, worn by the wife of Schliemann.
LEFT
Princess Morocco Berbere wearing a tiara on the day of her engagement.

FAR LEFT
Tiara by Lalaounis "Byzantine " style made in 22K gold precious stone.
LEFT
Tamil Nadu Bharata-natyan Swapna wearing traditional gold head ornaments set with rubies and pearls.
RIGHT
Princess Fawzia of Egypt on the day of her wedding. Parure and tiara by Van Cleef & Arpels.

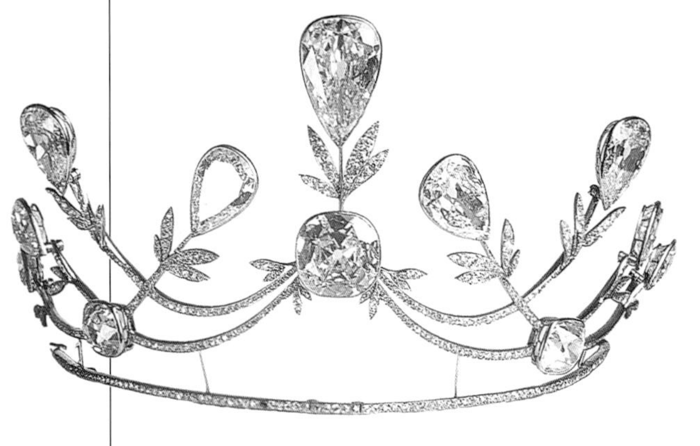

TOP LEFT
Empress Theodora and her courtiers are portrayed in this mosaic from 6th-century Byzantium.

TOP RIGHT
Sketch for a tiara by Boucheron.

INSET LEFT
The royal crown of the Qajar house of Persia includes about 1,800 pearls, 300 emeralds, seven large diamonds and 1,500 rubies and spinels.

INSET RIGHT
Wall painting from Pompeii, representing Briseis and Achilles who wears a tiara in pure gold.

CENTER
Imposing tiara in diamonds on platinum by Van Cleef & Arpels.

LEFT
Tiara with nine pear-shaped diamonds, Chaumet 1904.

stones, most notably garnets, emeralds, amethysts and pearls were featured. The Hercules knot or reef knot became the most prolific motif and the most popular style of headpiece — the diadem — was usually decorated with either a Hercules knot at the center or with a gable-shaped panel of embossed gold. The oriental diadem, seized on by Alexander, and consequently worn by the Hellenistic rulers, was resplendent with inlays of precious stones and colored glass.

That most exotic of cultural crossroads, India, with its vast variety of jewelry inspired by the rich diversity of the country's religious, social and ethnic influences, has pro-

duced some of the world's most exquisite head decorations. The cirdamani is a headdress made of precious stones; the muktajali is a hairnet fashioned from colored stones together with pearls. Kings wore tiaras composed from the amazing variety of Indian gemstones. The wearing of all jewelry was traditionally subject to a complex set of rules and infused with sensual power and cultured beauty.

ABOVE LEFT
Chinese Princess wearing a tiara made in gold thread and pearls, 18th century.

ABOVE CENTER
Tiara set with rubies and diamonds. Chaumet.

ABOVE RIGHT
Nadir Shah of Persia, who ruled from 1736 to 1747, conquered parts of the Mogul empire. Included in the booty he seized were jewels that once belonged to the great Aurangzeb and eventually became part of the Qajar crown.

RIGHT
The Goddesses Paramasukha-Chakrasamwara in cosmic union, 17th century Tibet.

Hair ornaments dominate China's contribution to jeweled creations. Typically, pieces feature lotus flowers combined with a silver dragon and two flying mandarin ducks on a fine mesh of silver wire. Other motifs include the simple plaited gold-wire hair pin and the phoenix bird perched on a slender pin, cut in silhouette from gold foil. The phoenix, originally the emperor's emblem, is considered particularly auspicious. Refined Chinese women of the Imperial Age also wore elaborate hairstyles highlighted with giant fan-shaped ornaments which encircled their heads like halos.

Crown jewels, always highly symbolic,

proclaim the wearer's sovereignty. Napoleon chose bees as his special emblem. Byzantine Empress Gisela, wife of Conrad II, used eagles to denote her imperial status. During the time of England's Henry VIII, soft velvet caps were worn by men both indoors and outdoors and were generally decorated with badges that ranged from simple gold buttons to elaborate jeweled masterpieces.

The imperial diadem, the sign of the ruler's dignity in the time of Constantine, was then a ring of jewels. Under Justinian, elaborate pendants, which hung down both sides of the emperor's head, were added. His wife, Theodora, wore a fabulous ring of precious stones and beads around her head, from which several strings of beads hung down to her chest, resembling strands of hair miraculously transformed into precious jewels.

Charlemagne's daughter, Rotrud, according to historian Angilbert, was perennially beautiful and lavishly

ABOVE
Tiara set with rubies and diamonds. Chaumet.

ABOVE LEFT
Queen Elizabeth I in 1585 wearing a tiara with pearls, rubies and emeralds.

CENTER LEFT
Empress Eugénie and the Dauphin.

CENTER RIGHT
Henry King of France, Navarre, with Queen Margot.

BOTTOM LEFT
England's Queen Mary had this diamond and pearl tiara designed for her in 1914.

BOTTOM RIGHT
Family tree of King Claude of France.

adorned: "her light shining hair is held by a blue ribbon, decorated with precious stones of luminous colors. She wears a golden headband decorated with beads." In contrast, Charlemagne himself donned a diadem for special occasions only.

TOP LEFT
The Empress Marie-Louise wears the pink topaz and diamond parure from her private collection.-Chaumet

TOP CENTER
Marie-Louise wearing the medallion sent to her in Vienna by Napoleon in 1810.

TOP RIGHT
Russian Tiara by Joseph Chaumet. This version of the kokoshnik is entirely paved with diamonds interspersed with pearls; surmounted by seven diamonds between pairs of pearls. It was executed for the wife of a Mexican millionaire.

UPPER RIGHT
Tiara for the Queen of France, Bourbon-de-Parme, Chaumet.

CENTER RIGHT
Philippe the First, King of France, with his wife Berthe of Holland, who wears a tiara in pure gold and diamonds.

LOWER RIGHT
The state crown of Queen Elizabeth was made for the coronation in 1937 of the present Queen Mother. The Koh-i-Nor was removed from Queen Mary's crown and placed here, where it remains today.

BOTTOM
Sketch for David's *Le Sacre de Napoleon I*, painted in 1805-7. With his left hand Napoleon holds the Consular sword, an allusion to the military victories on which his power was founded.

Queen Mary of Serbia, daughter of Kind Ferdinand I of Rumania and wife of Alexander I of Serbia, was obsessed with emeralds. Her favorite jewelry piece was a Russian tiara, known as a kokoshnik, which was one of the legendary treasures of the Romanov dynasty. Comprised of cabochon emeralds and diamonds, this supreme piece was created in the first half of the 19th century. Today it is a centerpiece in the private collection of Van Cleef & Arpels.

America's most famous first lady, Jacqueline Kennedy, wore diamond and platinum clips in her hair. Van Cleef & Arpels' most famous crown, fashioned for the coronation of the first Empress of Iran, Farah Pahlavi, was composed with a 150-carat flawless emerald, pear-shaped and round pearls, rubies and diamonds with claws of gold mounted on platinum. Britain's most famous princess, Diana, brought with her to the House of Windsor her family's most important heirloom: the Spencer Tiara.

FAR LEFT
Art Nouveau artists paid homage to feminine beauty.

LEFT
Princess Hyacinth. Alphonse Mucha. Prague 1911.

BELOW LEFT
Poster for Emmanuel Orazis. 1900.

England's Queen Elizabeth inherited a pearl tiara, made for Queen Mary in 1914, which she presented to Diana as a wedding gift. The tiara contains nineteen teardrop pearls. To commemorate her own marriage, Queen Elizabeth received from her father, King George VI, a sapphire and diamond tiara. So valuable is one royal tiara, now owned by Elizabeth, that an English aristocrat risked his life on its behalf, retrieving it from a St. Petersburg wall safe in 1917 after the Grand Duchess Vladimir of Russia escaped the Revolution, leaving it behind.

Not all royalty took their headwear so seriously. Diana's flair and originality got the better of her when she visited Emperor Hirohito of Japan. For that audience she wore an ostentatious watch and a handful of sapphires — gifts from the crown prince of Saudi Arabia — converted into a headband. More often than not, however, Diana's public appearances featured her most famous head ornament: her own natural, short blond hair. And with good reason. According to Andrew Morton, author of *The Wealth Of The Windsors*, "Time and again in the papers and diaries of members of the

ABOVE
This tiara, created by Chaumet, is a copy of the design Louis XVI made for the Marquise of Talhouet.

FAR LEFT
Designs for parures and tiaras. Chaumet.

LEFT
Zodiac Tiara. Alphonse Mucha. Paris 1896.

RIGHT
Tiaras. Boucheron 1920.

BELOW LEFT
Mauboussin's "Broche-Tiara," 1930. In diamonds, rubies and sapphires.

BELOW CENTER
Sarah-Bernhard wears a tiara of pearls and diamonds by Boucheron.

BELOW RIGHT
In a 1925 photograph by Cecil Beaton, Lady Wimborne wears a tiara in diamonds and rubies. Chaumet.

ABOVE
"Chanel Fringe." A spectacular piece in Coco Chanel's landmark exhibit in 1932.

BOTTOM CENTER
Platinum and diamond tiara and necklace worn on a model by Siegel. Boucheron, 1935.

BOTTOM RIGHT
Princess Felix Yussupoff, née Grand Duchess Irina of Russia, wearing an imposing diamond tiara in the form of an articulated sun, remounted by Chaumet in 1914.

royal family, references are made to the weight or discomfort of a crown — never to its worth or splendor." This tidbit explains the use of a prop at the investiture of Charles as Prince of Wales in 1969: "The glowing orb on his crown was, in fact, a table-tennis ball sprayed gold."

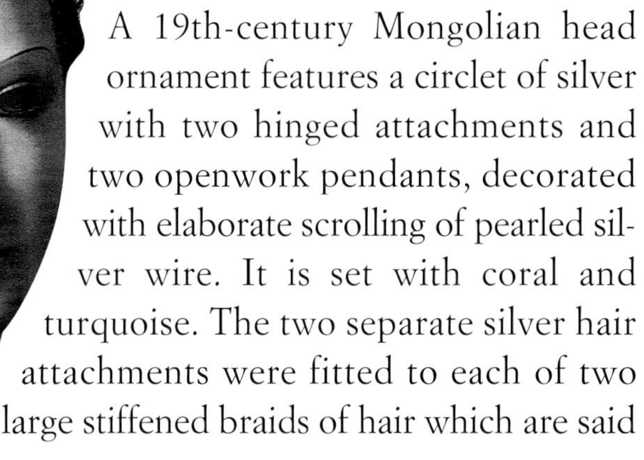

Even in countries known more for their spiritual than their material contributions to civilization, a decorated head is held in high esteem. Tibetan "ladies of good position" were known as Gyen-Sang-Ma, which means, literally, "she with good ornaments." A horned headdress indicated that the wearer was from the sacred capitol, Lhasa.

A 19th-century Mongolian head ornament features a circlet of silver with two hinged attachments and two openwork pendants, decorated with elaborate scrolling of pearled silver wire. It is set with coral and turquoise. The two separate silver hair attachments were fitted to each of two large stiffened braids of hair which are said

to represent cow's horns and serve as a reminder to married women of the Mongols' legendary descent from a nature spirit and a cow.

Tiaras (known in England as Spartan diadems), which rise to a point in the center, grew in popularity during the 19th and 20th centuries. In France, aigrettes made from colored stones were used particularly on turbans, while decorative combs, fashioned from tortoise shell or metal, were de rigueur daytime wear. It is believed that in addition to their aesthetic and symbolic significance, tiaras served a practical purpose as well: pulled tightly from the forehead back, tiaras smoothed out wrinkles and camouflaged other cosmetic flaws.

Even before Art Nouveau swept the world, bringing new attention to the art of jewelry design, the great houses of jewelry were established, setting the standard for beauty, wealth and

ABOVE
Lady Nutting "Parure Chaumet" tiara in diamonds, double pearl necklaces, and earrings in pearls and diamonds.

TOP CENTER
Miss Universe wearing a tiara.

TOP LEFT
Gouache painting of tiara for hair in yellow gold, diamond and color stones. Rene-Sim Lacaze, 1945.

INSET
At the premiere of *Lawrence of Arabia* in Paris in 1962, Elizabeth Taylor wore a diamond tiara that had been given to her by her late husband, Michael Todd.

CENTER
Tiara made in diamond swan motif that is detachable. It was worn by Grace of Monaco. Van Cleef & Arpels, 1965.

privilege. From Piccadilly to the Champs-Elysées to Fifth Avenue, the most prestigious jewelers competed to create crowning glories for the wealthiest, most prominent women in the world. In 1858, Fontenay conceived and executed an elegant diadem for the Empress Eugénie. Because the diadem had to be spectacular even when viewed from a distance, the jeweler designed a headdress with an arrangement offering two different aspects which could be altered at will. The nine large fleurons, enhanced with emeralds or sapphires, could be replaced with seventeen "large pendant pearls pointing downwards, which produced a lovely effect."

CLOCKWISE FROM ABOVE: A replica of Empress Farah Pahlavi's crown exhibited in a window of the Place Vendôme shop, the day of the crowning in Paris, October 26, 1967. Van Cleef & Arpels Archives.

Ludmilla Tcherina coiffed in a headpiece bordered by a row of brilliant diamonds and stuck with bird of paradise feather, studded with pieces of jewelry, circa 1960.

Sketch of the tiara Van Cleef & Arpels created for Queen Nazil for the wedding of her daughter Princess Fawzia of Egypt.

Dayle Haddon wears the "Tiara Papette" of flowers with 305 diamonds, Van Cleef & Arpels.

Princess Caroline of Monaco with her father, Prince Rainier. Caroline wears a Van Cleef & Arpels tiara.

Luis Bravo's partner wears a tiara while dancing the tango.

The tiaras of Chaumet perhaps epitomize the splendor of jeweled headwear. The diversity of designs, ranging from "the romantic princely and ducal crowns created for princesses and duchesses to the highly political fleurs-de-lis favored by supporters of the Bourbons in exile," Chaumet has created a design for virtually every occasion.

Maxim's de Paris, a Parisian restaurant so rich in Art Nouveau artworks that it has been dubbed "The Museum of Art Nouveau," was the center stage for socializing during that period. Maxim's was known as the place to meet the elite. Ladies bedecked themselves in their most opulent jewels. They were known as "High Priestesses of Love" and "women of ill repute" and in Maxim's they found a home. They formed a unique class of royalty. And in that vein, they wore the requisite tiaras, diadems, hair combs and headdresses. The well-known La Belle Otero was photographed in a bodice comprised entirely of diamonds and a pearl headdress, a striking contrast against her jet black hair.

TOP LEFT
Elizabeth Taylor at the Proust ball given in 1972 by the Baron and Baroness Guy de Rothschild. Her hair ornament forms a diamond net. Van Cleef & Arpels.

CENTER LEFT
Tiara made of diamonds. Piranesi.

LEFT
Diamond- and emerald-set platinum aigrette.

BELOW
Boucheron, 1958, illustrates a diamond festooned necklace of the era, worn as a tiara.

Art Deco's jeweled head ornaments, usually tiaras but also lighter aigrettes and bandeaux, remained an essential part of court and society dress in Europe. In 1921, these symbols of privilege also found their way into the annals of American royalty: the Miss America Pageant. On the Boardwalk in Atlantic City, the most beautiful girl was crowned with a sparkling, princess-like tiara. The women of wealthy industrial families — the Vanderbilts, Morgans, Goulds and Rockefellers — donned more majestic works of art: tiaras sculpted in diamonds and platinum.

A diamond diadem, draped across the forehead like jeweled bangs, was created by Gabrielle "Coco" Chanel in 1932. Embodying joie de vivre, the diadem was the perfect accouterment for a flapper's boyish locks.

American socialite Barbara Hutton was so fond of the tiara created for her by Van Cleef & Arpels — comprised of enormous pear-shaped diamonds as well as navette diamonds and brilliants — that she could not bear to take it off. Upon visiting her in her suite, where she was indisposed, Pierre Arpels was surprised to see Mrs. Hutton wearing her beloved tiara in bed.

Hollywood luminaries have claimed tiaras as their own. Gloria Swanson, at the 1950 Knickerbocker Ball, looked every bit as regal as any woman born to a throne with her hair lavishly swept under an enormous jeweled tiara. Joan Fontaine, Paulette Goddard and Catherine Deneuve all topped their exquisitely beautiful heads with priceless creations forged from precious metals and rare gemstones. At a 1972 "Proust" ball given by Baron and Baroness Guy de Rothschild, Elizabeth Taylor wore a spectacular hair ornament — virtually a net of diamonds covering a simple chignon.

Contemporary celebrities who have sported tiaras include Sharon Stone, Meg Ryan, Minnie Driver and Naomi Judd. Says Los Angeles jewelry designer Cynthia Bach, "There's a little princess in every girl and a tiara says it's wonderful to live the fantasy." And with the right accessories every grown woman can cast the glamour of a queen.

RIGHT
An 18K gold tiara with flawless diamonds, worn by Madonna. Gianni Versace.

Necklaces

Sparkling Promise of Romance

For anyone who thinks that a necklace is merely a piece of jewelry, consider this: A necklace may have contributed to the execution of Marie Antoinette. The world's finest necklaces claim not only great distinction but also prestigious residences, such as the Smithsonian Institute and the Louvre. Precious necklaces even have their own names: the Napoleon Necklace (a world-renowned diamond once owned by Marjorie Merriweather Post), La Peregrina (a pricey pearl once owned by Elizabeth Taylor) and Caesar's Ruby (oddly, an Indian pink tourmaline once a part of the Russian Romanov crown jewels). As jewelry's most flexible, most versatile piece, the necklace is head-and-shoulders above the rest.

ABOVE
Pierre Sterle Group 1960-1970 necklace featuring a stylised ginko flower. Chaumet.

FACING PAGE
Jewish Woman from Algiers. Eugene Delacroix 1834.

The story of the necklace begins before recorded history itself. As early as 30,000 BC, Paleolithic man and woman donned necklaces of stringed shells, carved bones, animal teeth and polished stone beads. More than one historian has pointed out that this prehistoric prototype essentially remains the basis for most of today's necklace designs. By about 2500 BC, the Sumerians were incorporating gold into their jewelry designs. Royal graves in Ur — today, Iraq — reveal necklaces fashioned from lapis lazuli and carnelian beads interspersed with gold wire components and leaf-shaped gold pendants. Chokers — short necklaces that tightly encircle the base of the neck — also seem to have been popular.

TOP LEFT
Moroccan woman wearing a pure gold necklace.

TOP RIGHT
Bracelet made in 24K pure gold, 1st century BC. Saint Raymond Museum, Toulouse.

CENTER LEFT
Necklace made in pure gold with rubies and stones from Africa.

CENTER RIGHT
A solid gold pendant of Tutankhamun wearing a string of glass beads around his neck. Metropolitan Museum of Art, New York.

BOTTOM LEFT
Scene from Egypt.

BOTTOM RIGHT
Serpent-shaped necklace in gold and diamonds. Gouache design, 1878. Boucheron.

Ancient Egyptian necklace design included pieces similar to those found in Ur as well as styles more particular to Egypt: the pectoral — the precursor to the pendant — and the elaborate broad collar. These collars, comprised of multicolored stone beads interlaced with gold, were so heavy that

ABOVE BACKGROUND
Necklaces in the Greek World from the 6th century BC onwards are amply represented as in this vase painting. The entire vase is shown at bottom.

ABOVE FOREGROUND
"Double-Axe." Gold necklace freely using the Minoan double-headed axe motif. Lalaounis.

CENTER
Gold parure in "exotic" style set with diamonds, rubies, white cultured pearls and hematite beads, 1948. Boucheron.

they required a counterbalance to offset their weight. The counterbalance, which held the collar in place, was made of strings of beads propped against the back of the wearer between the shoulder blades. Elements of nature that had magical or religious significance played central roles in all forms of jewelry. The scarab beetle, the most prevalent, represented the sun and creation. Lotus flowers symbolized resurrection. The colors of the stones used in jewelry designs were symbolic as well. Dark blue (lapis lazuli) symbolized the night sky, green (green feldspar) meant new growth and rebirth, red (carnelian) stood for energy and life. In one typical Egyptian design, road collar necklaces are comprised of bands of cylindrical beads arranged between two falcon heads. One such necklace, dating back to the end of the Twelfth Dynasty (1850-1775 BC), is made up of gold falcon heads and bands of

TOP RIGHT
The God of Bouray, 1st century AD, wearing a torque around his neck. Musée de Saint-Germain.

CENTER RIGHT
Necklace from the tomb of Princess Vix made in pure gold, 5th Century. Museum of Chatillon Sur Seine.

LOWER RIGHT
Painting of a Pompeii woman.

beads of gold, carnelian, turquoise and faience. More modest necklaces were made of colored stones or faience beads shaped into fish or flowers.

From Asia Minor across the eastern Mediterranean to Greece, gold was the most popular material for creating necklaces. Such goldsmithing techniques as granulation (the application of tiny golden spheres) and filigree (gold-covered beaded or twisted wire) were used in many of the artifacts found on the Greek islands. The most popular neck ornament was a collar fashioned from several gold plaques, either rectangular or trapezoid in shape, decorated with embossed figures and fitted with golden hooks intended to secure the wearer's dress at shoulder height.

Greek jewelry, necklaces in particular,

TOP LEFT
Polychrome enameled necklace with pearls, rubies, emeralds and sapphires set in 24K gold.

TOP CENTER AND RIGHT
Mughal ceremonial jewelry. Miniature paintings. Victoria & Albert Museum.

LOWER LEFT
19th-century gold necklace (gubluband), from Jaipur, Rajasthan, set with nineteen large, foil-backed diamonds, from each of which is suspended a large baroque emerald bead. Private collection.

ABOVE RIGHT
Gold necklace, 19th century, set with diamonds on enamel with emeralds, lower fringe polychrome enameled.

TOP
Necklace for the Contessa Camargo, design by Rene-Sim Lacaze, made of sapphire and diamonds, 1938. Van Cleef & Arpels.

CENTER INSET
Maharanee of Punjab.

BOTTOM CENTER
Maharaja Dhulip Singh of Punjab wearing his splendid crown ornaments and a diamond-framed cameo of Queen Victoria.

BOTTOM RIGHT
Masterpiece of Indian goldsmith's achievement. Gold necklace, 19th century, set with diamonds, pearls and fringe polychrome enameled on the back.

exhibited considerable artistic brilliance and quality workmanship during the 6th and early 5th centuries BC. There were as many as seven words for necklaces in the Greek language. The main styles of necklace included a row of gold sheet beads alternated with golden figurines and a row of flat elements offset by a three-dimensional pendant. During the Hellenistic period, a popular version was the strap necklace, consisting of ribbons of finely hewn gold chains linked together side by side supporting a fringe of small pendants. Cleavage-enhancing dresses encouraged new necklace designs. Broad collars worn at the base of the neck or tightly around it were actually inspired by the iron collars used for prisoners. However, unlike their metal counterparts, these exquisite necklaces were made of stones mounted on fabric

or gold and precious gems and fastened by ribbons tied at the back of the neck. Philip the Good, Duke of Burgundy in the 1390s, lavished his wife Marguerite with ruby, sapphire and pearl collars.

TOP LEFT
Marie Antoinette.

TOP CENTER
Charles X, the last Bourbon King of France, wearing a necklace set with "regent" diamonds.

ABOVE RIGHT
The Four Musketeers.

LEFT
A recreation of the sumptuous "Queen's Necklace" made of diamonds.

FAR LEFT
The Cardinal de Rohan, who was duped into taking part in the "Queen's Necklace" plot.

The more sophisticated the civilization, the more refined its jewelry. The pearl necklace is perhaps the signature of cultivation. Pearls were threaded into short chokers, multiple-rowed necklaces or long ropes. Sometimes these strings featured large gem-set pendants or pearl fringes in the shape of giant pearls. By the 17th century, the one thing all pearl necklaces had in common was that they were each fastened with ribbon ties.

During the early 18th century, women's fashions exhibited some amusing eccentricities. The panier skirt, for example, was so wide that two women could not sit on

the same sofa. Towering hairstyles were offset by plunging necklines. Neckerchiefs, consisting of squares of silk or muslin, were draped around the neck. Modesty pieces, also called tuckers, could serve as trimming along the edge of the bodice, augmenting the more risqué bodices. Necklaces were short and worn high on the neck, just under the chin, emphasizing the length and elegance of the wearer's neck.

In France, the most elaborate necklace design was known as the esclavage, consisting of the basic openwork band embellished with single or multiple central festoons

TOP LEFT

Collerette "Ingres" transformable brooch and earrings that can be worn as a necklace. Van Cleef & Arpels.

TOP RIGHT

Portrait of Princess D'Alice of Monaco wearing a dog collar.

LOWER LEFT

Chains of alternating emeralds and diamonds are intersected by seven large emeralds with a brilliant cut diamond border each hung with an emerald drop, the clap at the back is set with a square-shaped emerald.

LOWER RIGHT

Portrait of the Grand Duchess Stephanie de Beauharinais, niece of the Empress Josephine and adoptive daughter of Napoleon. Chaumet.

Countess de la Motte devised an elaborate ruse involving an unsuspecting Cardinal de Rohan to secure the necklace for herself. The

and gemstone pendants. One of the most extravagant and infamous esclavage necklaces was commissioned by Louis XV for his mistress Madame du Barry. This piece of jewelry was to provoke a scandal starring Marie Antoinette. After commissioning the necklace, Louis XV died before the piece was completed and paid for. The court jewelers, Bohmer and Bassenge, then tried unsuccessfully to sell the necklace to Louis XVI. The sinister Countess de la Motte devised an elaborate ruse involving an unsuspecting Cardinal de Rohan to secure the necklace for herself. The Countess, posing as Marie Antoinette, convinced the Cardinal that she wished to purchase the necklace without the King's knowledge. A forged note was given to the Cardinal. After obtaining the necklace, the Cardinal delivered it to the Countess, who made off to England with her lover to sell off the necklace piece by piece. Although Marie Antoinette and the Cardinal were both eventually exon-

ABOVE
Russian Princess, 1884.

TOP RIGHT
Spectacular diamond necklace mounted in platinum. Piranesi.

RIGHT
Marble of Princess Mathilde, cousin of the Emperor Napoleon III, wearing a necklace.

LEFT
Spectacular diamond choker by Boucheron, 1899.

BELOW
Heart-shaped necklace made of diamonds and rubies. Alexandre Reza.

LEFT
Queen Esther,
Leon Benouville, 1889.
RIGHT
Her Highness Seeta Devi, Maharani of Baroda, and her son Princie, 1948. She is wearing a matched set in engraved and round diamonds.
Van Cleef & Arpels

erated of involvement in the theft, it was widely believed that Marie Antoinette was somehow involved, contributing to her image problems with her countrymen. Ultimately their disfavor would lead her to the guillotine. The irony for the unfortunate Marie Antoinette is that the necklace she never even laid eyes on is forever known as the Queen's Necklace.

From across the English Channel another matriarch was to leave an indelible mark on necklace design: Queen Victoria, whose prudish personal taste in fashion, design, architecture and jewelry influenced all of Europe, and even for a time shifted leadership in jewelry design from Paris to London. Daytime fashions, replete with high collars, left little opportunity for wearing necklaces. Evening wear, however, still offered a bit of bare neck for adornment. Necklaces of the Victorian age were short, encircling the base of the neck and featuring frilly

ABOVE
Design for a necklace with rubies and diamonds.
LEFT
Necklace worn by the Empress Farah on the day of her coronation, set in platinum and gold with hexagonal emerald on the pendant: four emeralds, four pearls and eleven yellow diamonds in a diamond setting.
Van Cleef & Arpels

LEFT
Judith with the Head of Holofernes, 1900.

ABOVE
Necklace in 20-22K gold based on a decorative motif found on Minoan vases. Lalaounis.

ABOVE RIGHT
French writer Colette in her dance "Cleopatra."

designs: clusters of fruits and berries alternating with leaves, sprays of orange blossoms, roses and forget-me-nots. After their discovery in South Africa during the mid-1800s, diamonds began replacing all other gems, including pearls, as the most popular stone for jewelry, while silver temporarily supplanted gold. To maximize the dazzle of diamonds designers created a white-on-white effect with silver. Silver's use in this fashion, however, was short-lived. A large quantity was needed in order to keep the diamonds in place, making pieces heavy and cumbersome. Further to silver's discredit, it tarnished quickly, leaving marks on the wearer's skin and clothing. By the turn of the century, the pitfalls of silver were made inconsequential by the discovery of platinum.

Nature was a central theme during

ABOVE
A damselfly necklace of gold, enamel, aquamarines and diamonds (c. 1900-02). The delicate hovering insects are entwined to form curvilinear Art Nouveau shapes. Private collection.

FAR LEFT
La Belle Otéro wearing a dog collar and stem of pearls.

LEFT
An intricate gold necklace, decorated with turquoise-colored drops of enamel, set with brilliant diamonds and turquoises and hung with a single turquoise drop. 1958. Boucheron collection.

the Art Nouveau period. Animals and mythological creatures were often depicted in necklaces. Peacocks, swans, swallows, roosters, owls, dragonflies, butterflies, grasshoppers, bees, bats and wasps all starred in startlingly realistic depictions made possible by the enameling techniques used at the time. Egyptian scarabs, grasshoppers, chameleons, lizards, fish and seahorses were all popular figures for Art Nouveau jewelry. Such mythical beasts as Medusas, griffins, dragons and chimeras also frequently appeared dangling from golden chains around the necks of the women of Art Nouveau.

ABOVE
Necklace with a rare emerald center of 151 carats engraved on both sides, surrounded by diamonds and rubies. Alexandre Reza.

RIGHT
Illustration of necklace made of rubies, gold and diamonds. Mauboussin, 1942.

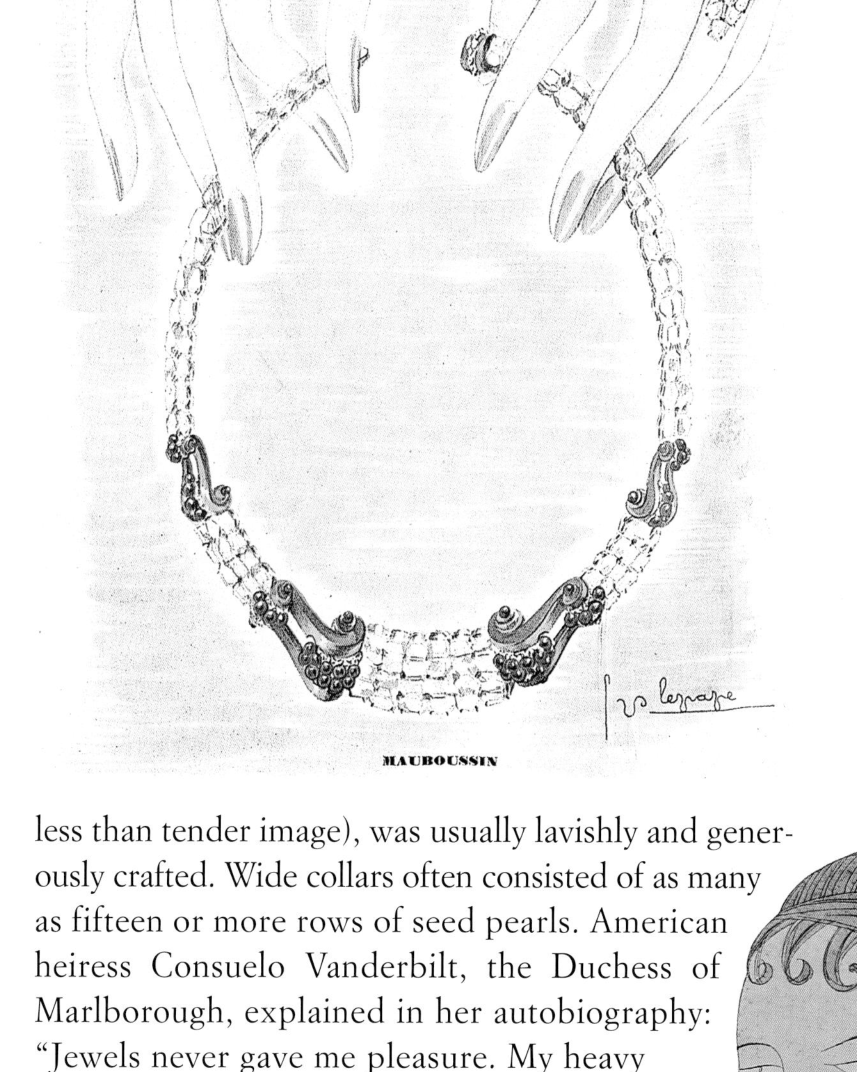

Women of the period often suffered in the name of beauty. The choker (whose name suggests anything but comfort), also known as the collier de chien (dog collar — conjuring a less than tender image), was usually lavishly and generously crafted. Wide collars often consisted of as many as fifteen or more rows of seed pearls. American heiress Consuelo Vanderbilt, the Duchess of Marlborough, explained in her autobiography: "Jewels never gave me pleasure. My heavy tiara invariably produced a violent headache. My dog collar chafed my neck."

But although the dog collar

BELOW
Necklace set in diamonds with a spectacular emerald. Piranesi.

RIGHT
Necklace made of diamond baguettes and pear-shaped emeralds, advertised for Van Cleef & Arpels, 1930. Harper's Magazine.

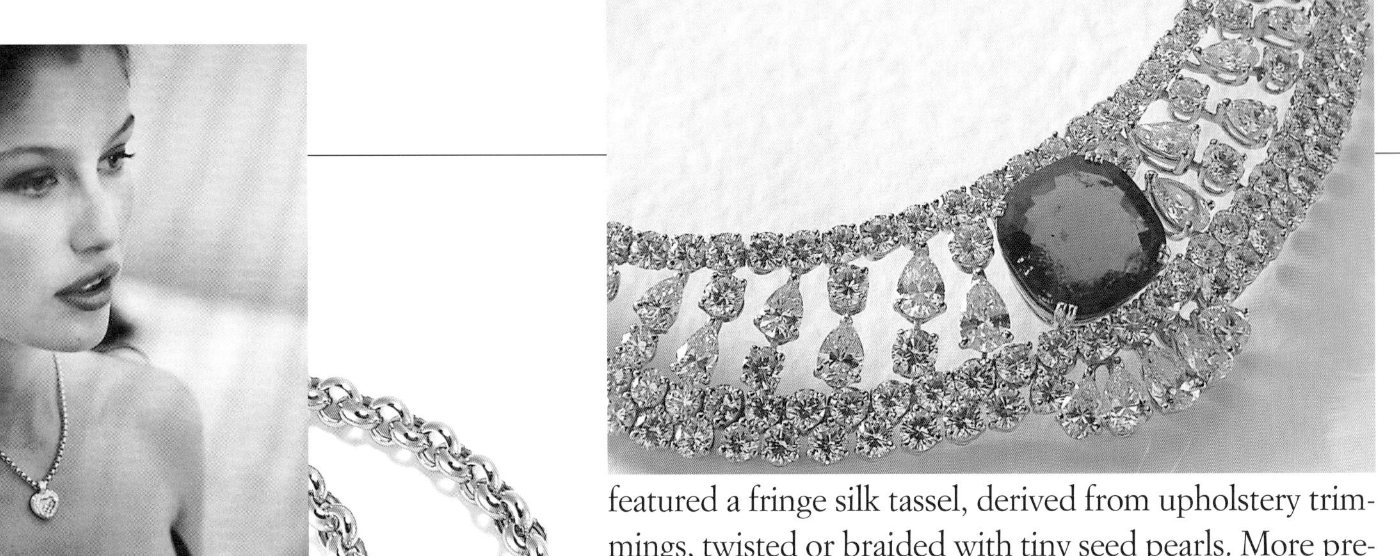

featured a fringe silk tassel, derived from upholstery trimmings, twisted or braided with tiny seed pearls. More precious pendants were made up entirely of such stones as diamonds, coral, onyx and pearls. "America's Sweetheart," cinema star Mary Pickford, sported a forty-inch sautoir comprised of two strands of three-millimeter pearls as her favorite daytime accessory.

was not the most comfortable of accessories, it did serve a practical purpose on occasion. Queen Alexandra wore one to cover a small scar on her neck.

A ubiquitous feature of late-19th-century necklaces was the rivière (stream), featuring stones mounted in open-backed collets. These were held by claws supported by a metal arched structure. This setting type worked particularly well for diamonds.

The sautoir, a long necklace often made up of many strands of pearls, decorated with diamonds and ending with one or two tassels is most illustrative of the Art Deco necklace. The customary sautoir

In that time of prodigious innovation and inspired artistry, all the leading Parisian jewelry design firms — Boucheron, Cartier, Chaumet and Van Cleef & Arpels — created enduring works of Art Deco. Stones were combined as never before — precious and semi-precious side by side. New diamond cuts were introduced: trapezes, semicircles, darts, barrels and triangles. In the wake of the global economic crisis that followed the 1929 Wall Street crash, the world of jewelry continued to thrive. Short necklaces once again reigned supreme. In 1936, the Duke of Windsor, still King Edward VIII at the time, purchased from Van Cleef & Arpels a

TOP LEFT
Laetitia Casta, L'Oreal ambassadress, wearing a Chopard Happy Diamonds pendant. Photo: Steve Luncker

TOP CENTER
Happy Diamonds. Heart-shaped pendant in white gold, entirely set with diamonds, 12 moving diamonds. Chopard.

TOP RIGHT
Necklace with an emerald center, diamonds set on platinum and gold. Boucheron.

FAR LEFT
Eva Herzigova wearing Chopard Haute Joaillerie. Photo: Christian Coigny

BOTTOM
Marilyn Monroe.

RIGHT
Heart-shaped necklace made of emerald with a chain made of diamonds. Piranesi.

FAR RIGHT
Cover of *l'Officiel*, 1963. Woman wearing a pearl necklace.

LOWER RIGHT
Gold three-part serpentine necklace with cabochon saphires and diamond brilliants set in platinum. Van Cleef & Arpels, 1949.

spectacular Burmese ruby and diamond necklace as a 40th-birthday gift to Wallis Simpson. Deeming the necklace too ordinary, the Duchess of Windsor returned the necklace to the jeweler to have it reset in a completely different style.

World War II had a devastating effect on production of fine jewelry. The use of gold was restricted. Platinum was banned entirely for use in jewelry. Diamond supply from South Africa was irregular and other precious stones were scarce as well. To meet the constant demand for jewelry, large semiprecious gems — aquamarine, amethyst, citrine and topaz — were favored. Necklaces were most often short and fashioned from flexible tubular gold bands in two predominant styles: the "snake chain" of interlocking links, and "gas pipe linking" in which two long strips of gold with raised edges were wrapped around a removable core. In 1939, Van Cleef & Arpels' passe-partout necklace epitomized gas-pipe linking. The necklace was so flexible it could also be worn as a bracelet.

In the '50s, Hollywood glamour was all the rage. Necklace designs were curvilinear, fluid, asymmetrical and, above all else, feminine, emulating the figures of the women who wore them. Pearls, popularized by Coco Chanel during the halcyon days of Art Deco, enjoyed a rebirth. In addition to the single strand, multiple strands

of pearls set with diamonds were in vogue. Prince Rainier of Monaco, in 1956, gave just such a necklace to his bride, Grace Kelly, as a wedding gift.

Necklaces paved no new ground during the '60s, while the '70s brought a reappearance of the sautoir. But it was during the decade of decadence that the necklace once again claimed its power. While in the past, women primarily received jewelry as tokens of love or symbols of the status of their spouses, during the 1980s, with their newly-acquired financial independence, women began buying jewelry for themselves. Bold designs eclipsed more delicate creations. Huge "South Sea" pearls were perfect for the larger-than-life quality women sought. And, of course, reflective of the conspicuous consumption that characterized the '80s, spectacularly expensive and luxurious necklaces with enormous pendants of precious stones were very popular.

The scaled down '90s have brought restraint to jewelry design in general and necklace styles in particular. Styles favor simplicity. And while no one can predict what the next trend in necklaces will be, one thing is certain: With more than 30,000 years of history, the necklace is here to stay.

TOP LEFT
Coco Chanel wearing strings of pearls.

TOP RIGHT
Cabochon necklace made of rubies, pearls and diamonds mounted on gold. Piranesi.

BELOW
Necklace with diamonds and pearls. Alexandre Reza.

FACING PAGE
An Etude of diamonds and rubies by Boucheron.

9369
14218
142463
16854
9038
3096
305563
36
9037
9060
16881
9444

Earrings

Dropping Suggestions at Every Length

Framing the face with a dazzling sparkle, dangling to enchanting lengths, occasionally brushing delicately against the neck — earrings are as delightful to the observer as they are to the wearer. Subtler than the tiara or crown, earrings also draw attention to a woman's face, but with less flash and ostentation. Yet for a truly spectacular effect, earrings can be coordinated with a necklace, bracelets, rings and brooches. When modesty is a must, the sophisticated woman ensures that, at the very least, her necklace matches her earrings.

ABOVE
Egyptian earrings in gold.

LEFT
Cat Goddess, Egypt, 600 BC, in bronze. Earrings in gold.

FACING PAGE
Frieze from the Palais of Artaxerxes.

Earrings have a history of their own, as old as the brooch, as rich as the bracelet. Pierced ears date to nearly 900 BC in Western Asia. Clusters of beads, hollowed out in order to hide perfumed oils, were popular in the third and fourth centuries BC. In Ancient Rome, "auricolae ornatrices" — experts on the complications suffered by women from the prolonged wearing of large and heavy earrings — were highly regarded. And, according to ancient historian Pliny, "Women liked to wear earrings set with two or three pearl drops that rattled at the slightest movement of the head."

Because of the elaborate hairstyles, headdresses and high-collared costumes that characterized the Middle

COUNTERCLOCKWISE FROM ABOVE

Ear pendants in 22K gold featuring rosettes from the Hellenistic period with chains encircling sodalite, medallions with lyre motif inspired by Homer. Lalaounis.

Portrait in wax of a Roman woman wearing gold-and-pearl earrings.

Hermes wearing earrings and a Chalmyde.

Portrait from the 4th century. Roman women who wore pearl earrings in public asserted their high social standing.

Sculpture from the tomb of Palmyra of a woman wearing several necklaces, earrings and brooches. This fashion was very popular throughout the Roman Empire in the 2nd and 3rd centuries.

Ear pendants inspired by artifacts in the Museum of Persian Jewelry, 22K gold. Lalaounis.

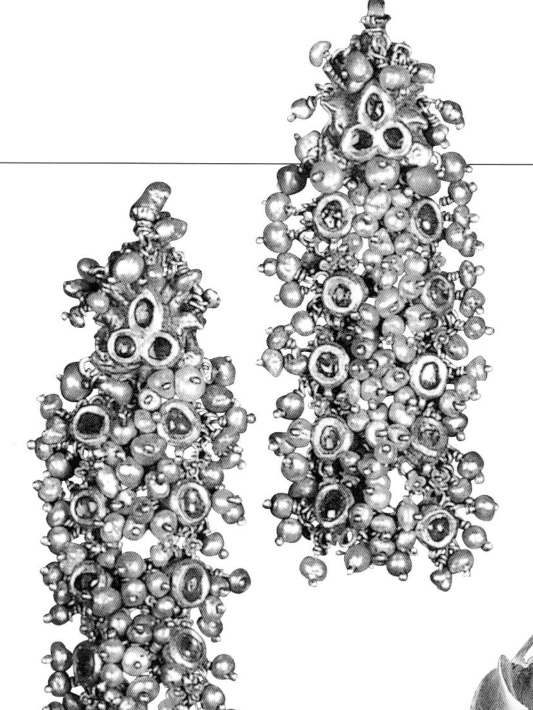

LEFT
Pendant earrings from India date to the late 19th century. Gold setting with pearls, rubies and emeralds.

RIGHT
The Goddess Tara from Tibet. The Cleveland Museum of Art.

BELOW
From the Peules women in Mali. Earrings in pure gold. The size of the earrings represent the wealth of the family.

Ages and the Renaissance, earrings were a well-kept secret during those times. In the 19th century, as hairstyles became more down-to-earth, earrings enjoyed a resurgence. A parure created by Lucien Falize in 1887 features a gold necklace and matching pierced earrings, the earrings hung with pendants centered on enameled portraits painted by Alfred Meyer. By the early 1900s, pierced ears were considered barbaric and the clip-on claimed the limelight.

RIGHT ABOVE
Earrings from a tribe in Borneo, representing "aso," a dragon who deters evil spirits.

RIGHT BELOW
Gold earrings from the Shunga Dynasty. The Cleveland Museum of Art.

FAR RIGHT
Empress of China, wife of the Emperor Shiht'su, wearing pearls and ruby earrings. Yuan dynasty, 1277.

Ornate earrings, dangling and jeweled, were the preferred accent for the new short hairstyles of the Art Deco era. Long pendants culminating in cascades of diamonds and bunches of fruit in engraved stones were the perfect complement to boyish cropped locks. Boucheron created

ABOVE LEFT TO RIGHT

On the small island of Flores, different tribes wear this earring style. They are often given as a wedding gift.

Konyak Naga wearing ear ornaments comprised of the brilliant, feathered wings of the Indian blue jay.

Gold earrings worn by a cheif of the Masai.

RIGHT

Rai Marsum tribal woman wearing silver top ear studs. Her lobe is distended by a silver loop.

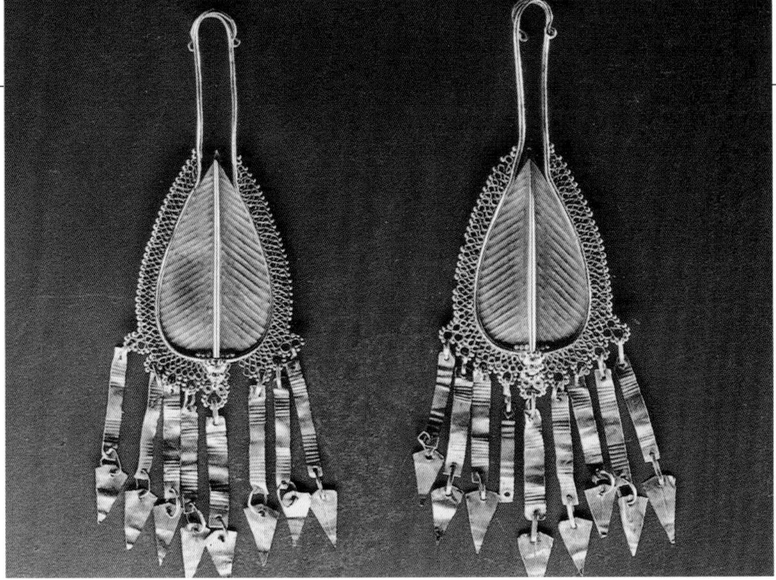

long earrings capped off in drops of pearls as well as a series of pendant earrings in drops of onyx, jade, cornaline and brilliants. Cartier's 1924 pendant earrings were composed of emeralds, pearls and brilliant-cut diamonds, mounted on platinum.

For her marriage to the Infante of Spain, Princess Alice de Bourbon-Parme wore a parure comprised of diamonds and rubies set in platinum designed by Chaumet. Giant blood-red rubies radiated from the Princess' royal ears. The Duchess of Windsor wore a parure, necklace and earrings of faceted rubies and diamonds, created by Van Cleef & Arpels, to the International Cannes Film Festival in 1938. Mauboussin made the "Lattice" parure in yellow gold. The detachable round clip is fastened to a latticework chain, with matching ear clips formed of delicate gold wire accented with rubies and pear-shaped aquamarine stones. Bulgari was a favorite destination of Andy Warhol, who said, "When I'm in Rome I always visit Bulgari,

LEFT TO RIGHT

Tibetan warrior wearing a long silver Kham earring with a large coral bead.

Earrings worn by the chief of an African tribe, the design symbolizes male sexuality.

Earring ornament in Ivory from the sea near Marquise Island.

African "Ancestor" figure, Baluda, 19th century.

because it is the most important museum of contemporary art." The jeweler showcased a positively hypnotic parure, as colorful as a peacock's tale: A necklace with matching pendant earrings, dating from the late 1950s, featuring cabochon-cut sapphires, rubies and emeralds set amid brilliant-cut diamonds.

Coco Chanel, who was just as likely to wear plastic as she was platinum and pearls, fashioned matching earrings, brooches and necklaces from gold, mother-of-pearl and silver. Paloma Picasso has been captured by the camera wearing an elaborate Tiffany parure of necklace and earrings set with a wide selection of precious and semi-

CLOCKWISE FROM LEFT
Gold earrings from Suba in pure gold.

A ball at the court of Henry the IV. Many of the men wore earrings during this period.

Richard Sackville, Count of Dorset, known for wearing only one earring.

Pendant ear clips with spectacular cabochon cut rubies surrounded by pavé diamonds. Bulgari.

Painting of an odalisque. Eugene Delacroix, 1815.

Portrait of the Infante Isabelle of Spain.

22K gold earrings. Lalaounis.

RIGHT
Spectacular earrings with baguette diamonds with emeralds, canary yellow diamonds and two round-cut diamonds. Alexandre Reza.

BELOW
Versace earrings, diamonds mounted in yellow gold.

BELOW RIGHT
Diamond pendant earrings set in platinum. Van Cleef & Arpels.

FACING PAGE
Sophia Loren, Sharon Stone and Jacqueline Kennedy Onassis wearing earrings by Van Cleef & Arpels.

precious stones, her signature "X" backlit with diamonds.

Contemporary parures may be created with turquoise and diamonds set in platinum, as in the case of Chaumet. Or they may be diamond stud earrings paired with a solitary diamond threaded through a thin gold chain. Simple solo pearls can be matched with a strand coiled delicately around the neck. And when all else fails, gold hoops can sensuously highlight an earlobe and match any gold necklace. Certainly, earrings are not a necessity. But how many women would dare leave home without them?

Brooches

Hopes Pinned On Precious Gems

THE JOURNEYMAN OF JEWELS, THE BROOCH IS NOT JEWELRY FOR JEWELRY'S SAKE. Oh, the five-inch flamingo flashing from the bodice of Wallis Simpson's suit may look frivolous. But be assured, it is not. Perhaps it holds, just so, a scarf. Or a fragile ego, as in the case of Paulette Goddard who received from Charlie Chaplin a pair of cabochon emerald and diamond clips as consolation for losing the part of Scarlett O'Hara. Or could it be that beautiful jeweled creations — pinned strategically below sensuous collarbones — conceal the real family jewels? For the 1948 film *The Three Musketeers* Lana Turner and Angela Lansbury wore brooches known as the "Cleavagels" to pacify film censors who deemed their partially exposed bosoms too risqué for the public eye.

ABOVE
Diamond and gold brooch with a spectacular "pigeon blood" ruby. Alexandre Reza.

FACING PAGE
Brooch by Van Cleef & Arpels, 1981. The scarf is a Gruau creation.

The brooch's beginnings are humble. While necklaces, earrings and rings serve no function, the brooch, like all firstborn, has responsibilities. It was created to hold clothing in place. It is, in effect, the precursor to the button, the zipper. Before magical amulets, before symbols of union or power or prestige, before any other piece of jewelry, there came first the brooch. Yet, long after intricacy and sophistication were laced into most other jewelry pieces, brooches remained uneventful circular discs. Women wore paired brooches on their shoulders to secure simple tubular dresses. Togas, if you will. Occasionally a string of beads was hung between them. By the

ABOVE
Art Deco "Egyptian Warrior" brooch, platinum, diamonds, rubies, emeralds and onyx. Chaumet, 1924.

FAR LEFT
Egyptian Prince

UPPER INSET
Etching depicting King Tutankhamun and his queen.

LOWER INSET
Greek amphora.

BOTTOM
Brooches from the Vercingetorix period, 60 BC, in pure gold.

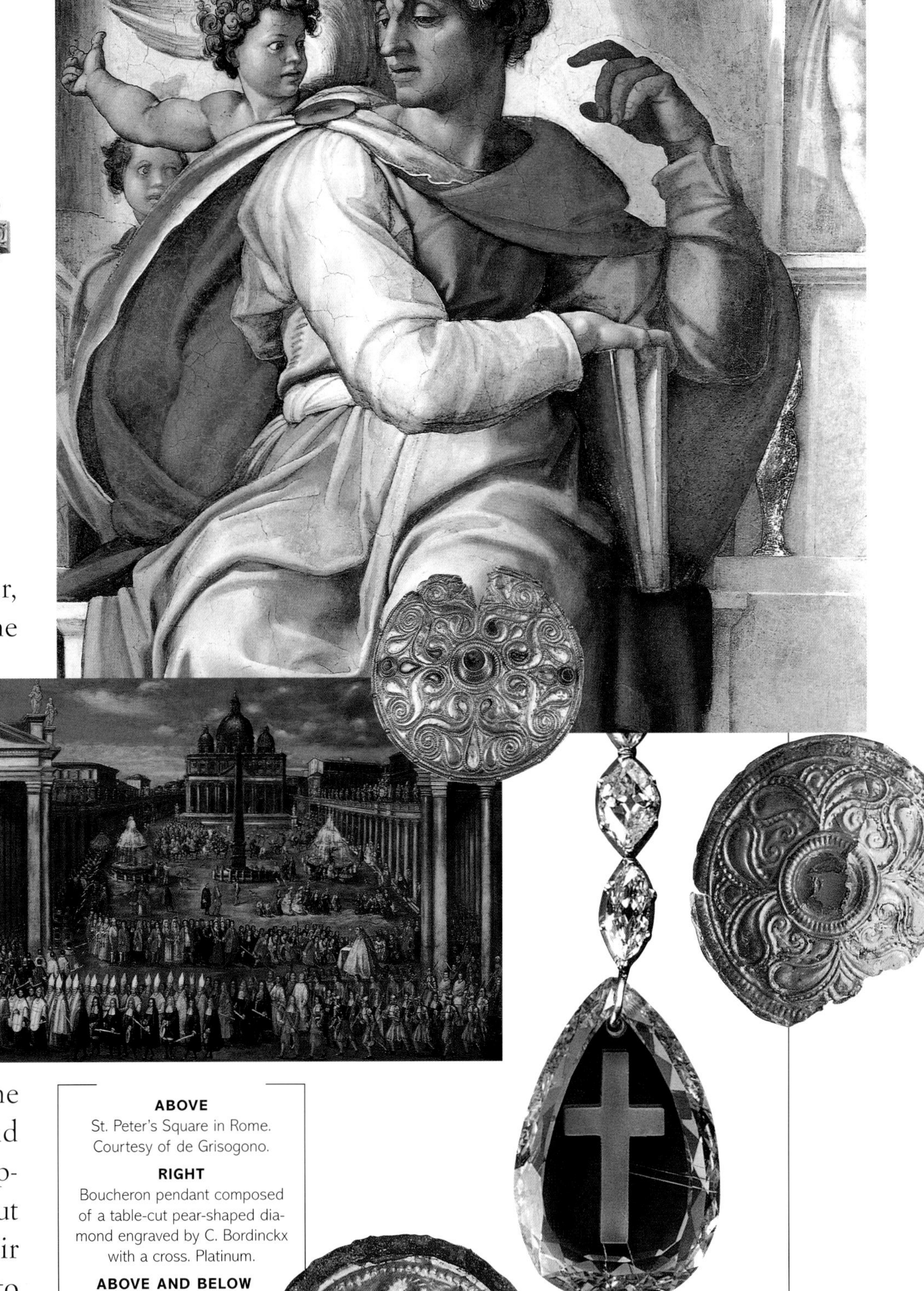

ABOVE
Brooch in 18K gold with an "arcade" reminiscent of mosaic technique. The rubies, emeralds and sapphires recall the wealth of colors seen in art during the Byzantine period. Lalaounis.

TOP RIGHT
Scene from the Sistine Chapel. Vatican Museum.

mid-6th century, however, brooches were allowed to shine in their own right. A pair of Visigothic eagle-shaped fibulae of gilt bronze, rock crystal and colored stones adorn the framework of metal cloisons. A 7th-century gold disk brooch found in Bavaria is decorated with beaded wire and inlaid garnets that form a pattern of interlaced double-headed serpents.

As with all other forms of jewelry, each civilization has put its own spin on the brooch. Celts favored the penannular brooch throughout the early Christian and Viking periods. An early Slav cast-silver bow brooch typifies a Ukrainian style. The ancient Chinese tended to put more jewelry in their hair than anywhere else on their bodies. But the Colombians place first when it comes to

ABOVE
St. Peter's Square in Rome. Courtesy of de Grisogono.

RIGHT
Boucheron pendant composed of a table-cut pear-shaped diamond engraved by C. Bordinckx with a cross. Platinum.

ABOVE AND BELOW RIGHT
Three brooches made in pure gold, dating to the 5th century BC.

the most unusual place to wear a brooch: the nose. One example from c. 500 AD features a nose ornament, covering the entire lower half of the face, cut from sheet gold. Because of the thinness of the gold and of the attachments, which are suspended from wires, the whole piece would have trembled when worn. The ornament was worn through a perforation in the nasal septum.

ABOVE
Elephant made in diamonds and pearls. Piranesi.

LEFT
Japanese hair brooch, 18th century. Cloisonné design with diamonds, rubies and pearls.

The brooch has played a role in a gruesome event. In one classic tale, an Athenian expedition attempting to conquer the neighboring island of Aegina met with resounding failure. Only one Athenian man survived the foray. Upon returning home to Attica, the soldier was met by the wives of his slaughtered compatriots who were livid about the death of their husbands and decided to take revenge on the only survivor. The women removed the brooches that fastened their dresses and one by one struck the lone soldier, each in turn demanding to know where her husband had been left. The man did not survive this experience, and as punishment for their crime, the women were forced to abandon their style of dress in favor of linen tunics that did not require brooches.

ABOVE
Brooch of two lizards in diamonds and rubies. Chaumet.

ABOVE RIGHT
Pierre Sterle Group brooch featuring a flying hummingbird with a lapis lazuli body, diamond-studded crest and gold wings. Chaumet.

RIGHT
Butterfly brooch with four wings made in diamonds, engraved by C. Bordinckx, the body composed of a cushion-shaped ruby and a faceted, pear-shaped diamond. Boucheron.

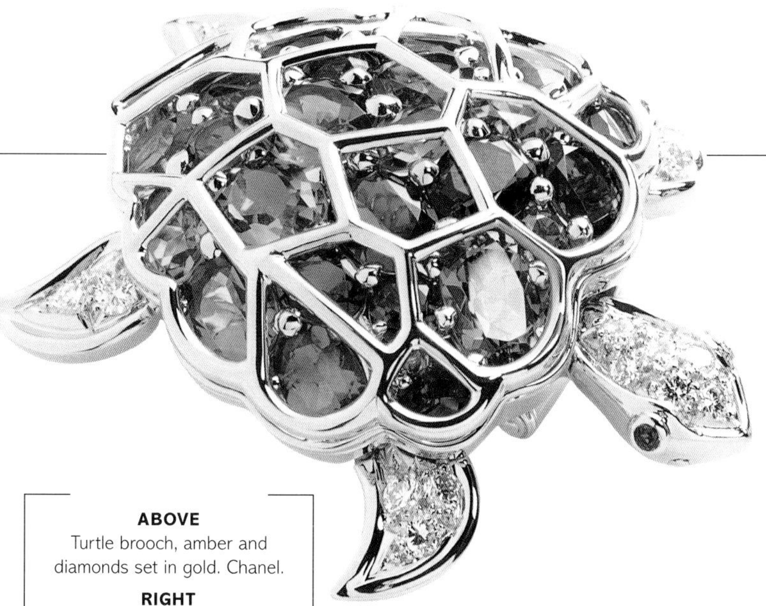

ABOVE
Turtle brooch, amber and diamonds set in gold. Chanel.

RIGHT
Two dramatic Boucheron brooches. (Above) A jackal's head is crowned with the heads of two serpents, in chased gold. The jackal has ruby eyes; its jaw grasps a brilliant diamond from which a fine round pearl is suspended. 1900. (Below) Two serpents glare at each other with emerald eyes as they battle over a garnet, set in gold.

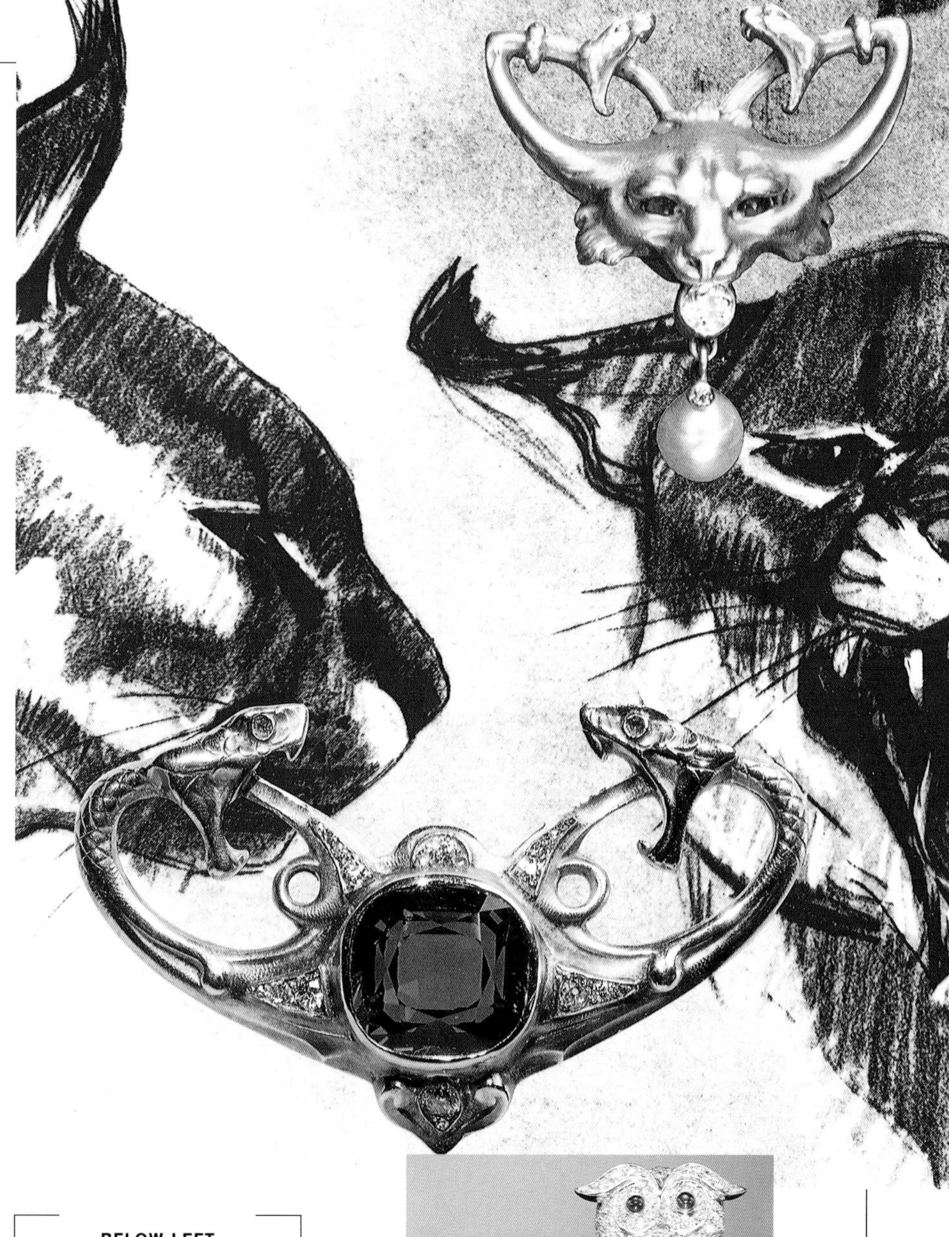

Animals have always been a favorite theme in the world of jewelry, and for brooches in particular. For the ancient Egyptians, the scarab beetle represented the sun and creation. According to Richard Hattatt, author of Ancient and Romano-British Brooches, "All animal brooches have the pin pointing towards the head, and all the flat plate type have the head facing to the right." Like the brooch itself, the reason behind this is practical: "Since most people are right-handed, in fixing the brooch with the right hand, it is pushed to the left with an upward tendency. If the creature were reversed on the pin, the tendency when worn would be for the rump to be higher than the head." Clearly, a no-no.

The presence of animals on jewelry is often symbolic. A lamb carved on any stone was long thought to protect the wearer against palsy. Stags, the ancients believed, cure lunacy and madness. Comedienne Joan Rivers relates a story about another kind of symbolism. In her personal jewelry collection, Rivers counts a "very romantic brooch given by Edward VII to his mistress, Mrs. Keppel. It's

BELOW LEFT
Panda brooch made in 18K gold set with black, white, cognac and pink diamonds, by de Grisogono.

BELOW
Porcupine brooch made in gold, pearls, and diamonds, nose of onyx. Chanel.

RIGHT
Owl brooches from the "Pietra Dura" collection. Piranesi.

FAR RIGHT
Owl in gold with sapphires, rubies and diamonds, sits on a gold and emerald branch. Alexandre Reza

an enormous red tourmaline encircled by a diamond snake. Though the brooch is extraordinarily opulent, its symbolism is what makes it special. Think of it: A rare, fiery gem (Mrs. Keppel, I presume) is embraced by a snake wrapped around itself — a symbol of eternal love — yet the snake's head is facing outward in a protective posture. Such passion!"

FAR LEFT
Brooches made in emeralds and diamonds worn by Maharaja Dhulip Singh of Lahore, 1852.

LEFT
Spectacular brooch from Tibet made in gold with turquoise and rubies.

In direct contrast to the oversize painting-style brooches characteristic of the early 20th century, at the end of the 19th century small brooches were worn scattered all over the bodice. In the 16th century, a typical Spanish bodice ornament, fashioned from gold, diamonds and emeralds, was set on springs so that it would quiver as the wearer moved. A German stomacher brooch comprised of brilliant-cut diamonds and pearls from the same era covered the entire front panel of the bodice and was made in two parts to allow for movement.

ABOVE
Brooch from India, 16th century, made in rubies, emeralds and diamonds.

LEFT
Brooch as used in a hair ornament, made in pearls, rubies and gold.

RIGHT
Brooch with a large sapphire surrounded by diamond and ruby petals, rising into an emerald, ruby and diamond plume. West Bengal, c. 1757.

FAR RIGHT
Marlene Dietrich's brooch, featuring pavé-set, half-moon, circular- and baguette-cut diamonds centering on an oval cabochon mounted in platinum. Mauboussin.

More than a few brooches are as famous as the luminaries who wore them. The "Sévigné" brooch, set with antique Colombian emer-

ABOVE
Large "passe-partout" bouquet made of four blue Ceylon sapphire flowers, with centers of faceted rubies, and leafs, sterns and tie in polished gold. Van Cleef & Arpels, 1940.

RIGHT
Portrait of Princess Henckel von Donnersmarck. Chaumet.

FAR RIGHT
Napoleon I in 1810, bedecked with diamonds for the occasion of his second marriage, to the Archduchess Marie-Louise of Habsburg. Chaumet.

alds, was designed for the illustrious 17th-century author, the Marquise de Sévigné. A clover-shaped brooch presented by Napoleon III to his wife, the Empress Eugénie, upon the birth of the Imperial Prince in 1856, is another piece of historical importance. Even before the brooch's reemergence in the 20th century as the diva of jewelry pieces, by 1897, as Queen Victoria celebrated sixty years on the throne, it was customary to bestow upon travelers to London, prior to their trip, a pink Jubilee enamel brooch. The Tiffany orchid, an amazingly realistic depiction of "Schilleriana" found in Brazil, put the American jeweler on the map internationally.

RIGHT
Platinum clip set with brilliant- and baguette-cut diamonds. Christie's documentary photo, 1950s.

FAR RIGHT
Portrait of the Duchess of Windsor painted by Gerald Brockhurst. She is wearing one of her favorite brooches: a large bouquet of sapphires and rubies set in gold.

The Victorians, not noted for their frivolity, nonetheless were as smitten

TOP LEFT
Illustration from *La Gazette du Bon Ton*, 1925. Boucheron.
CENTER
Oval watch in Chinese style; brooch in jade, coral, onyx, lapis-lazuli, diamonds and pearls. Mounted in gold and platinum. Boucheron.
TOP RIGHT
Illustration from *La Gazette du Bon Ton*, 1900. Boucheron.
BELOW
Double brooches made of baguette diamonds and emerald-cut. The brooch transforms into a bracelet. Van Cleef & Arpels, 1932.

with symbolism as earlier societies. While a wide selection of jewelry was available to commemorate an engagement, wedding or the birth of a child, the choice of an important piece for the mother of an established family proved to be more difficult. One solution: turquoise, diamond and ruby bluebirds with their chicks perched, mouths wide open, on a golden branch. Gold swallows gathered on a diamond-set perch conveyed an entirely different message: migration to warmer climes — from New York City to Palm Beach, perhaps.

Russian-born Princess Bagration used her inheritance to finance her jewelry acquisitions. A portrait of her shows an enormous sapphire securing a delicate white garment about her creamy shoulders. The Baroness James De Rothschild was known for her great fashion sense when it came to jewelry. With pearls lining the entire front of her bodice, she capped off her accessories with a Pompadour-type Sévigné brooch. And the jeweler responsible for the exquisite creations adorning these ladies: Chaumet.

During the 1920s, an era dominated by flapper style, brooches were the most striking complement to Coco Chanel's ingenious invention-the little black dress. Shimmering

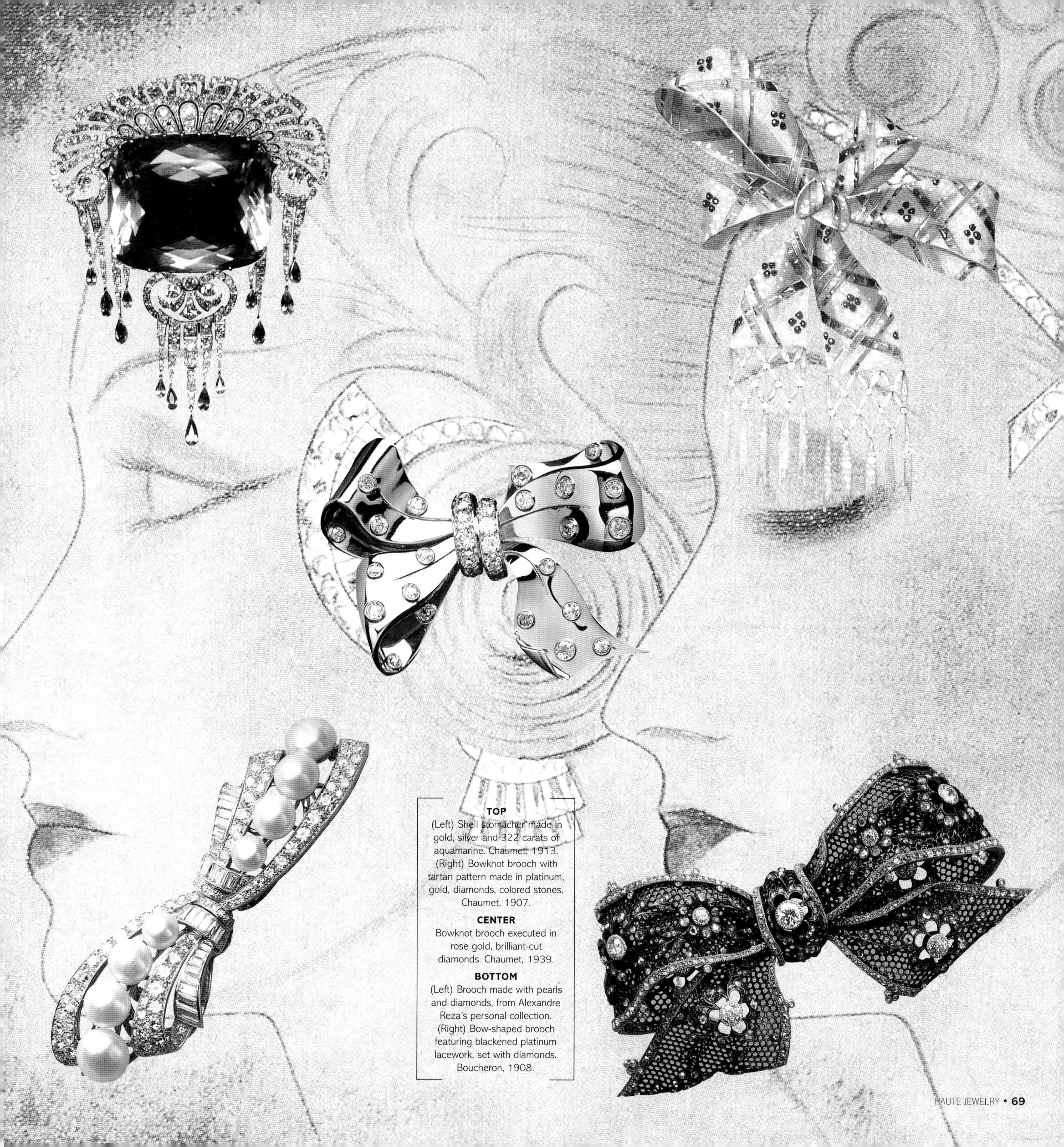

TOP
(Left) Shell stomacher made in gold, silver and 322 carats of aquamarine. Chaumet, 1913.
(Right) Bowknot brooch with tartan pattern made in platinum, gold, diamonds, colored stones. Chaumet, 1907.

CENTER
Bowknot brooch executed in rose gold, brilliant-cut diamonds. Chaumet, 1939.

BOTTOM
(Left) Brooch made with pearls and diamonds, from Alexandre Reza's personal collection.
(Right) Bow-shaped brooch featuring blackened platinum lacework, set with diamonds. Boucheron, 1908.

diamond stars, accented here with an emerald, there with a pearl, were favored by Chanel. Beyond the jewels that adorned the bodices of her dresses and exquisitely tailored suits, Chanel often wore a beret accented with a brooch.

FAR LEFT
Model wears a double brooch made in diamonds. Mauboussin.

LEFT
Bellini brooch created in platinum and diamond. Van Cleef & Arpels.

CENTER INSET
Brooch made for Paris International Exposition, 1937. Mauboussin.

BOTTOM LEFT
Three brooches set with rubies, sapphires, and diamonds made for the New York World's Fair, 1939. Boucheron.

BOTTOM CENTER
Branch of white and black pearls on gold. Tina Segal.

BOTTOM RIGHT
"Liberation Jeep" in gold, rubies, sapphires and diamonds. Mauboussin, 1965.

Chanel's friendship with jewelry designer Fulco di Verdura inspired some of the most spectacular brooches ever pinned to a frock, a collaboration between two avant-garde artists: "Effigy" executed in sapphires, diamonds and emeralds, and "Rose" featuring sumptuous naturalism, are just two examples.

Reinvented by the great jewelry houses during the Art Deco era, brooches were the perfect canvas for whimsy, allegory, geometry. The brooches of George Fouquet from that period seem as contemporary today as they did nearly eight years ago. Van Cleef & Arpels popularized the dancer clip and then took the motif one step further. America's preeminent ballerina, Suzanne Farrell,

performed bedecked in diamond-laden golden masterpieces. Princess Anne-Marie of Denmark was frequently spied wearing her Van Cleef & Arpels "Swan" clip.

Perhaps more than any other jeweler, Van Cleef & Arpels explored one of the most dynamic characteristics of the brooch: its versatility. The "Passe-Partout" or "Multi-Purpose" brooch, comprised of a gold serpent chain and one or more brooches, could be worn in various combinations — as necklace, bracelet, brooch or belt ornament. At the heart of the design is that most stable of jeweled accessories: a brooch that could adjust the length and positioning of the serpent chain. The corolla-shaped brooches, in yellow, pink and blue Ceylon sapphires, were detachable and could be worn on the lapel of a suit

ABOVE
Brooch in diamonds on platinum. Advertisement published in *Plaisir de France* (June and September 1951). Boucheron.

TOP RIGHT
Diamond brooch.

BOTTOM RIGHT
Gianni Versace's signature "Medusa" brooch.

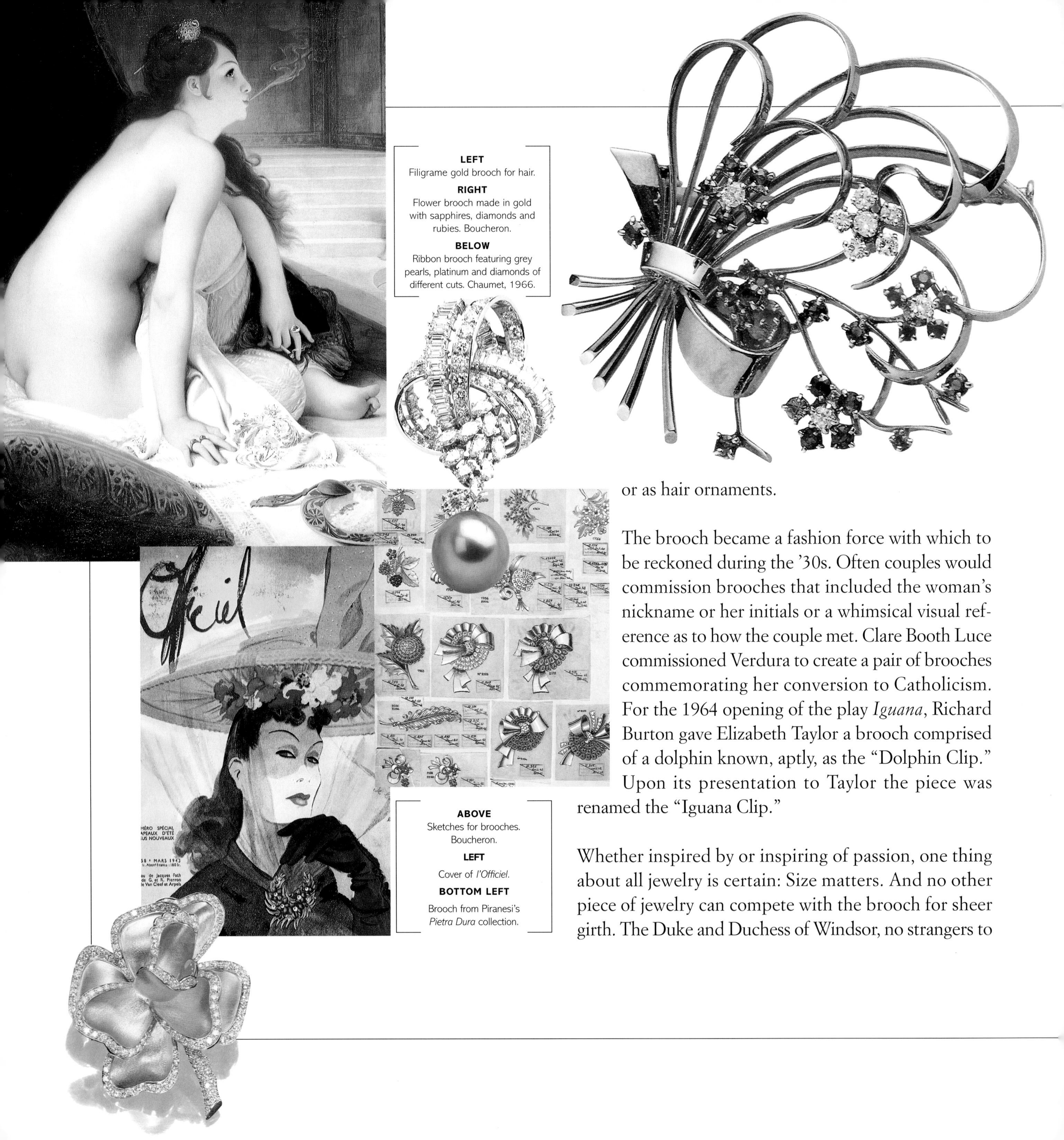

LEFT
Filigrame gold brooch for hair.
RIGHT
Flower brooch made in gold with sapphires, diamonds and rubies. Boucheron.
BELOW
Ribbon brooch featuring grey pearls, platinum and diamonds of different cuts. Chaumet, 1966.

ABOVE
Sketches for brooches. Boucheron.
LEFT
Cover of *l'Officiel*.
BOTTOM LEFT
Brooch from Piranesi's *Pietra Dura* collection.

or as hair ornaments.

The brooch became a fashion force with which to be reckoned during the '30s. Often couples would commission brooches that included the woman's nickname or her initials or a whimsical visual reference as to how the couple met. Clare Booth Luce commissioned Verdura to create a pair of brooches commemorating her conversion to Catholicism. For the 1964 opening of the play *Iguana*, Richard Burton gave Elizabeth Taylor a brooch comprised of a dolphin known, aptly, as the "Dolphin Clip." Upon its presentation to Taylor the piece was renamed the "Iguana Clip."

Whether inspired by or inspiring of passion, one thing about all jewelry is certain: Size matters. And no other piece of jewelry can compete with the brooch for sheer girth. The Duke and Duchess of Windsor, no strangers to passion or opulence, illustrated the brooches' potential for magnitude. In 1948, the Duke commissioned for his wife a panther brooch. The brooch consisted of this feline fashioned in speckled gold lolling atop a cabochon emerald weighing 116.74 carats. This three-dimensional panther was groundbreaking for Cartier. The following year, the Windsors purchased a cabochon sapphire weighing 152.35 carats and again commissioned Cartier to create the second of the now-famous Panther Brooch series. The sapphire was decorated with a seated panther interspersed with sapphires and diamonds.

Unlike other jewelry pieces, the brooch is not for everyone, nor is it worn for all occasions. Most often, the brooch is for royalty, real or imagined, the wealthy and the stylish. Yet brooches have come a long way, from the 7th-century BC and a silver and parcel-gilt Etruscan comb-fibula used to fasten coarse woolen cloaks to a Fred Leighton seven-inch, 37-carat diamond dragonfly brooch worn by Sharon Stone as clasp for her Vera Wang sarong at the 1998 Academy Awards. Worn routinely, as well, by such celebrities as newscasters Cokie Roberts and Jane Pauley, brooches may be particularly practical in history and in provenance; they do have, however, great style.

ABOVE
Aquamarines and citrines set in gold. Chanel.
RIGHT
L'Africain, Henri Matisse

Bracelets

Declaring Spirit and Style

Even the smallest gesture becomes a glittering ballet of movement with a bracelet adorning the wrist. If one's audience isn't already captivated, a jeweled arm in a sweeping motion is sure to command attention. The bracelet was born at least six thousand years ago, and was perhaps the first statement of pure fashion. Unlike the brooch, the origin of the bracelet does not derive from practical use. Unlike the ring, the bracelet is not richly endowed with symbolism. The very essence of fashion, the bracelet has remained, to a great extent, unchanged. In fact, a gold reef-knot bracelet from a four-thousand-year-old grave at Mostagedda, in modern day Egypt, is virtually indistinguishable from today's familiar love-knot design.

ABOVE
Gold bracelet from the region of Brasov, Transylvania. There are only three examples of this type of bracelet. Vienna Museum.

FACING PAGE
Sardanapale.
Eugene Delacroix, 1827.

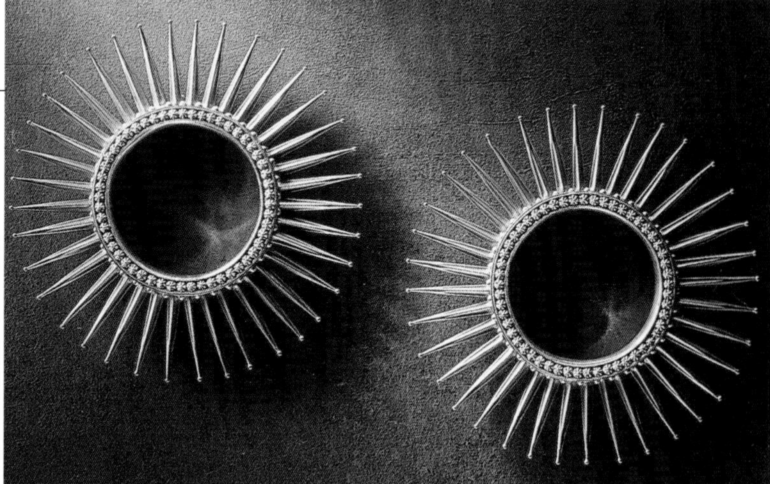

The earliest designs to dangle from the wrist included beaded bracelets and bangles. Ivory bangles, dating to 4000 BC, have been discovered on the body of a three-year-old child. Seemingly worn only by males, they are typical of the kind of bangle common to the period. In the Ur tomb of the zealously accessorized Queen Puabi, pairs of hollow bracelets were made of hammered sheet gold.

TOP LEFT
Juda and Thamar.
TOP RIGHT
Ankle bracelets in pure gold from Africa.
CENTER LEFT
Angami Nagas at a festival wearing brass armlets and bracelets.
CENTER RIGHT
18th-century anklet from the Ghysels collection, Brussels.
BOTTOM LEFT
Goda-Baca Indian anklets ornamented with decoration balls.
BOTTOM RIGHT
Pair of dyed canework cuffs ornamented with shells.

Ancient Egyptian bracelets were fashioned from beads of amethyst, carnelian, lapis lazuli, green feldspar and turquoise. They were strung on gold or gilded silver. Bangles of this period were made from a thin strip of sheet gold beaten into shape on a wooden ring and soldered together. Broad cuff bracelets were inscribed with stories. Panels depicting gods, serpents and lotus flowers were cast in pairs of bracelets. Not all bracelet designs were restricted to the wrists: beaded links sensuously adorned the ankles, and, as in the case of Cleopatra,

banded rings of gold called armlets encircled the upper arms as well as the wrists.

King Tutankhamun, in 1336 BC, wore gold bracelets inlaid with colored stones and glass fashioned into scarab beetles. At about the same time, west of Egypt, on the Mediterranean island of Crete, the Minoans favored bees and honeycombs as the basis for jewelry designs.

In Greece, jewelry enjoyed a Geometric Period from about the 11th to the 8th century BC. The simple lines of the designs created patterns that were as intriguing as they were elegant. Contemporary Greek goldsmith Ilias Lalaounis has refashioned a number of these ancient designs, dubbing them Neo-Geometric. With computer-enhanced precision, a repeated pattern of 18-karat gold squares is centered on a solid square of full-cut diamonds to

ABOVE
Gold bracelet with a ruby and pearls to be worn at the top of the arm. Devoted to the cult of Shiva.

TOP RIGHT
Queen of Assyria.

LOWER LEFT
Anklets from Sudan, Africa.

LOWER RIGHT
Anklets from Africa.

BOTTOM
Rigid silver anklet from Punjab.

create an exquisite bracelet.

Iron Age armlets (1st and 2nd century AD) were cast complete as hoops with relief ornaments. The open terminals of the enormous pieces were decorated with roundels inlaid with red and yellow champleve enamel. Bronze armlets found at Castle Newe, Strathdon, Aberdeenshire are decorated with a checkered pattern.

During the Byzantine era, the fashion of wearing pairs of bracelets emerged. Bangles comprised of panels of gold incorporating sentimental inscriptions were common. The most distinctly Byzantine style was made with a large hoop and a central roundel with a hinge on one side and a clasp on the other. Both the roundel and the hoop were decorated, either in plain gold or with settings of precious stones and pearls. A golden bracelet from 6th century Constantinople is decorated with pearls, sapphires and green chalcedony.

A lavishly decorated silver hinged bracelet from the 12th or 13th century found at Kiev bears motifs that include

ABOVE
Scene from Egypt, 1877.

CENTER LEFT
Pure gold bracelet from the tomb of Allenluften, 6th century BC.

CENTER RIGHT
Bracelet in 20-22K gold recalling the finest period of Egyptian art.

LOWER LEFT
Bracelet in the Egyptian style, decorated with lotuses and a serpent. Gouache design by Paul Legrand. c. 1870. Boucheron archives.

BOTTOM
Egyptian bracelet. Sapphire, rubies, diamonds and onyx mounted in platinum. Van Cleef & Arpels.

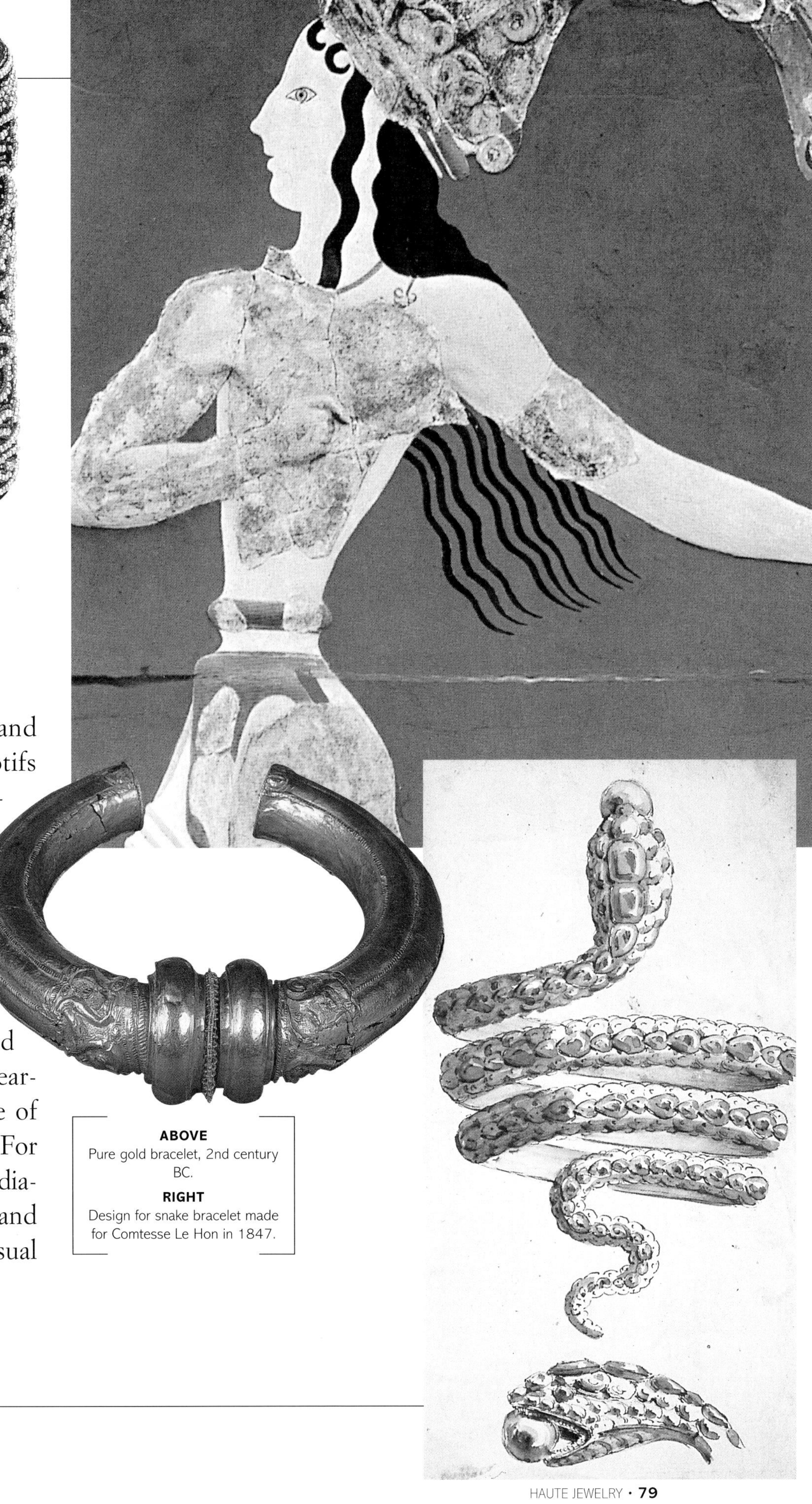

ABOVE
Ecclesiastical cuffs made in red velvet and solid seed pearl embroidery and gold spangles. 17th century Moscow.

TOP RIGHT
Prince from Crete, 4th century BC.

birds, fish, a mythical creature and intricate foliate forms. These motifs are pagan in origin and were standard wear at the time for wealthy Russian women. In China, during the same time, armlets wound from above the elbow to the top of a woman's arm. And bangles made from pure jade were, as they are today, considered most auspicious.

From the 1790s well into the 19th century, jeweled bracelets often doubled as love notes. Terms of endearment were often spelled out using the "language of stones," or the initial letters of particular gemstones. For example, the word "Dearest" would be comprised of diamond, emerald, amethyst, ruby, emerald, sapphire and topaz. This style of bracelet gave birth to many unusual

ABOVE
Pure gold bracelet, 2nd century BC.

RIGHT
Design for snake bracelet made for Comtesse Le Hon in 1847.

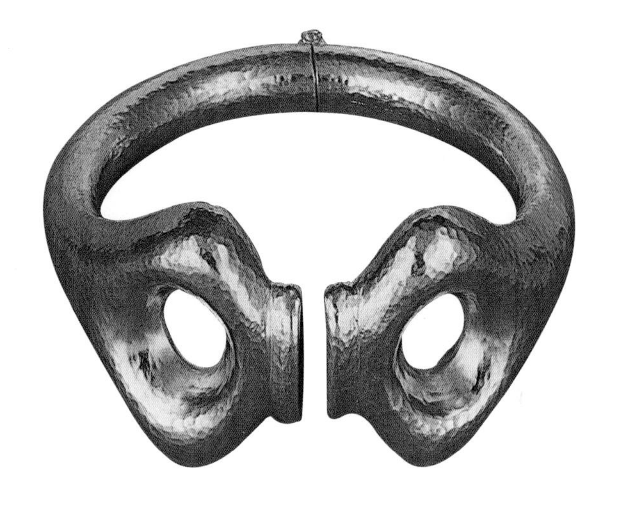

color combinations. Marie-Louise, wife of Napoleon, had three such bracelets made. One represented Napoleon's birthday, one her birthday and the third was inscribed with two dates: the day they met and the day they married.

By the mid-19th century, new styles of bracelet were gaining favor: linking bracelets sporting huge jeweled clasps worked their way up the arms of those who could afford them.

One of the world's most dramatic bracelets was created in 1899. The jeweler Georges Fouquet and the artist Alphonse Mucha worked together to create from gold, diamonds, rubies and a mosaic of opals a serpent bracelet and connected ring for the actress Sarah Bernhardt.

With the advent of Art Nouveau, natural motifs became more popular in bracelet designs. Foliage, depicted with realistic detail, entwined around ladies' arms. Snakes slithered. Birds and bugs alit on branches, fluttering into motion with each hand gesture. A Fouquet bracelet of the era features a leaf

FACING PAGE

TOP LEFT
Pure gold bracelet from the Phoenician Royal Tomb, 6th century BC.

TOP RIGHT
Bracelet in 20-22K gold inspired by an anthropomorphic terracotta vase of the late Neolithic (second halfof the 4th millennium BC) from Cyprus.

CENTER
Three twisted gold charnieres, separated by gold wire, also twisted, form the main body of this bracelet, which ends in ferocious lions' heads, of18K gold and precious stones.

RIGHT
Goddess Athena, 6th century BC. Archeological Museum, Athens.

BOTTOM
Three gold bangles with sapphires and diamonds on the left. A greek scene engraved on a bracelet, between two diamond bangles. All in 18K gold. Doris Panos.

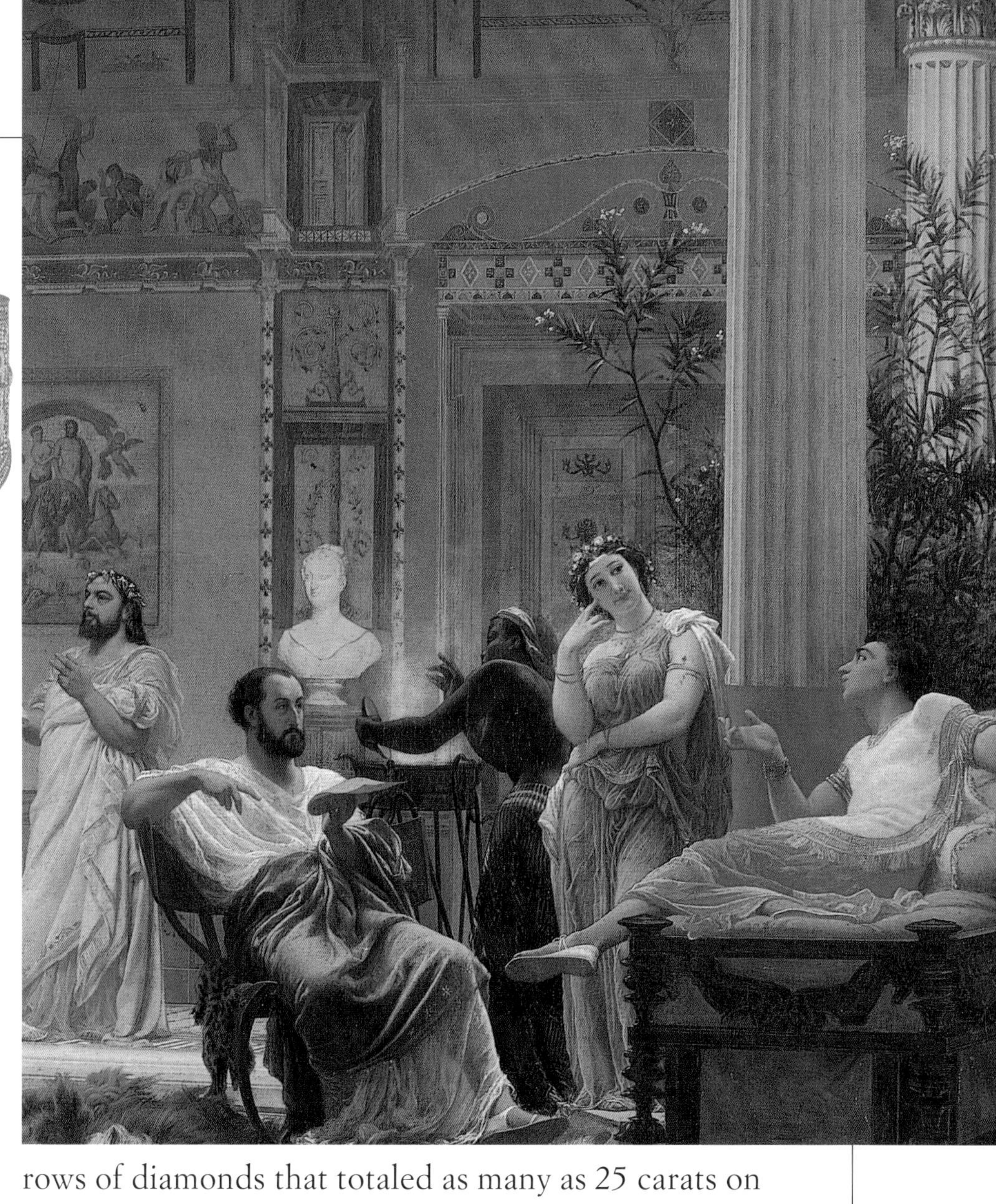

joined by turquoise cabochons that were selected for the black matrix they contain. The bracelet is highlighted with pearls and a small diamond in each link.

The fashions of the Art Deco era contributed to even greater creativity in bracelet design. Short-sleeved and sleeveless frocks inspired numerous new designs and styles of bracelets. Bangles, worn on both the upper and lower arms, were extremely fashionable. Flexible platinum-and-diamond bracelets were also in high demand. Styles ranged from a straight, single thin row of diamonds set in platinum to wide rows of diamonds that totaled as many as 25 carats on platinum. Often these white-on-white diamond-and-platinum bracelets were accentuated with rubies, sapphires and emeralds. At the Exposition des Arts Décoratifs of 1925, Van Cleef & Arpels won a prize for a bracelet set with delicate roses, diamonds and rubies interlaced with emerald leaves.

ABOVE LEFT
Bracelet in 20-22K gold and sodalite. The symbol of eternal friendship is beautifully decorated with granulated gold. Lalaounis.

ABOVE
Scene in Rome.

LEFT
Sword in silver. Lalounis.

BELOW
18K gold and diamond bangles. Doris Panos.

For her publicity photographs from

ABOVE LEFT
Woman from North India wearing abundant geometric bracelets.

ABOVE
Jewelry found in the tomb of Princess de Vix, 5th century BC. Archeological Museum, Chatillon-sur-Seine.

the '20s and early '30s, Joan Crawford wore multiple wide, Art Deco bracelets. Peggy Hopkins-Joyce wore calibré-cut sapphires and rubies mounted in platinum. American jewelers, not known as particularly fine cutters or designers, were nonetheless brilliant mechanics. They created (and patented) flexible mountings for line bracelets. The line bracelet was a simple way of showing off a row of calibré-cut gems perfectly matched in color and size. In the United States, they were nicknamed "Service Stripes" for two reasons: because they resembled the chevrons worn on military uniforms, and because they were often bestowed upon wives engaged in successful marital "tours of duty."

A sapphire and diamond chain bracelet with the center link sculpted into a star motif appears airy and delicate, even fragile, but the minute platinum links render the piece practically indestructible. When England's Edward VIII abdicated the throne in favor of marrying American divorcée Wallis Simpson, wedding rings and a bracelet celebrating the stages of their romance were crafted by Cartier out of platinum. In the film *Public Enemy* (1931), Jean Harlow wore a gem-set diamond and platinum bracelet.

TOP
Brahman bride receiving wedding gifts from the groom's family.

ABOVE
Elephant, body in sterling "nielle", setting in pearls and precious stones.

BELOW
Rigid gold bangles, Varanasi, 19th century.

ABOVE
Pair of pearl and gold bracelets from India.

RIGHT
Emerald and diamond bracelet. Alexandre Reza.

BELOW LEFT
Traditional, pure gold bracelet worn by the Bugis women at their weddings. Indonesia.

BELOW RIGHT
Minakshi-Devi (the fish-eyed goddess). The Hindu practice of decorating the image of a deity with jewelry is believed to make its beholding a great pleasure and blessing.

In *The Great Ziegfeld* (1936), a wide, Art Deco diamond bracelet plays a supporting role on the wrist of Anna Held (played by Luise Rainer). Fanny Brice, whose comedic gifts coupled with her charming femininity made her the quintessential Ziegfeld girl, once complimented Averill Harriman's wife on her diamond and emerald bracelet. A few weeks later, Harriman sent Brice a similar piece. For her portrait in *Vanity Fair*, Brice wore, among other pieces, a gem-set bracelet.

"The language of stones" bracelet made a comeback under the name "phrase jewel" during this era. In a black-and-white lobby card for the film *Desire* (1936), Marlene Dietrich wore her cabochon emerald bracelet by Trabert & Hoeffer-Mauboussin. Even without the color there was no mistaking the identity of the gem in her bracelet. The world's most famous recluse, Greta Garbo, made famous (or infamous, as the case may be) the machette, or cuff bracelet, highlighted with sapphires and baguette, round- and square-cut diamonds and designed by Van Cleef & Arpels. That firm also introduced the supple, or "Ludo" bracelet, made from thin gold rectangular panels in a brickwork

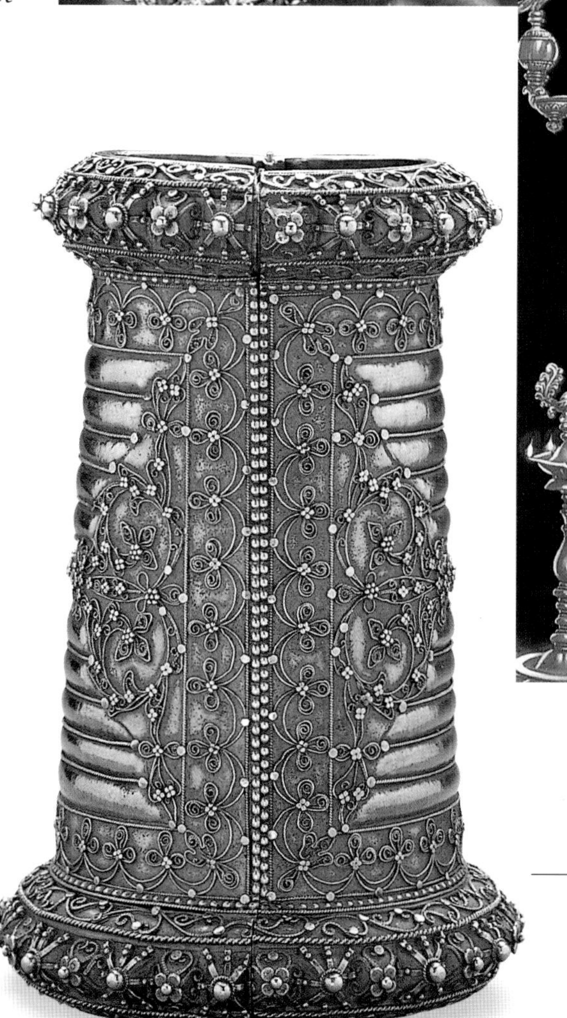

bracelet clasp was decorated with cabochon rubies and round diamonds. The "Ludo" bracelets were named affectionately for Louis Arpels whose nickname was "Ludovic."

In a 1932 Photoplay article entitled "Spend!", Joan Crawford declared herself the ultimate consumer: "I, Joan Crawford, I believe in the Dollar. Everything I earn, I spend." This, it bears pointing out, was amid the depths of the Great Depression. In pursuit of this philosophy of unbridled hedonism, Crawford worked her way into the very select clientele of New York jeweler Raymond C. Yard, a firm famed for never advertising. She walked away with a wide fancy-cut diamond bracelet highlighted with star sapphires. The center stone weighed 73.15 carats and the two side stones 63.61 and 57.65 carats. The bracelet became the star of her fabulous collection of cabochon sapphires that the press dubbed "Joan Blue" in her honor.

LEFT
Alphonse Mucha, 1897.
TOP RIGHT
Art Nouveau bracelet created for Sarah Bernhardt in 1899.
LOWER LEFT
Sketch of Aphrodite by Bernardo Buontalenti for the 1589 Italian opera *La Pellegrina*.
LOWER RIGHT
Lattice diamond mounted in platinum cuff. Piranesi.

Gloria Swanson wore a pair of platinum, rock crystal and diamond bracelets designed by Cartier. The diamonds are cut in brilliant and

TOP
Marlene Dietrich wearing Mauboussin.

CENTER
Greta Garbo as Maria Walewska in *Conquest* (1937), wearing antique matching bracelets composed of rubies, emeralds, sapphires, amethyst, topaz, and black and white enamel mounted in gold.

LOWER LEFT
Art Deco bracelet of rubies and diamonds. Chaumet.

LOWER RIGHT
Diamond and platinum bracelet made in 1925. Cartier.

baguette shapes. Created without clasps, they can be slipped on by means of a clever mounting on platinum springs.

Prince Rainier of Monaco ordered a stunning diamond and pearl parure that included a bracelet as a wedding gift for Princess Grace. The National and Municipal Council also gave the former Grace Kelly a spectacular gift: a bracelet with five rows of diamonds designed in kind by Van Cleef & Arpels. Maria Callas, Elizabeth Taylor, Christina Onassis, Barbara Hutton, the Vanderbilts, Mellons, Kennedys, the Duke of Westminster, the Aga Khan, King Farouk and the

Maharajah of Baroda have all dangled from their celebrated wrists spectacular jewels created by the Arpels.

During the 1980s, tricolor gold (yellow, white and rose) was very popular in all types of jewelry. Such surface-coloring techniques as patination (antiqueing) and enameling in opaque black and in rich jewel-toned reds, blues and greens enabled jewelers to achieve a heavy metal look with gold. One stunning example is the "Metropolitan Collection," an ebony 18-karat gold bangle bracelet from the Italian firm La Nouvelle Bague. Cartier reintroduced in platinum the "Rolling Rings" style of rings and bracelets. The original golden version was created for the poet Jean Cocteau.

TOP LEFT
"Viking" bracelets, 1951. Mauboussin.

TOP RIGHT
Bracelet with semiprecious stone setting in gold and diamonds. Van Cleef & Arpels.

CENTER
Bracelet in 18K yellow gold. Alexandra Reza.

BOTTOM
"Ivy" bracelet in yellow gold, rubies and diamonds. Boucheron.

FACING PAGE
"Gioia" bracelet in yellow gold with semiprecious stones. Chaumet.

While the most important gems are usually reserved for the necklace, the bracelet claims sensuality as its own: the lyrical jingle of bangles and charms, the tinkling of silver and gold bands caressing each other. The bracelet is elegant, frivolous, sensational, yet modest at times, sneaking up the sleeve of jacket or blouse. Ultimately, the bracelet is fashion's finishing touch. As comedienne Joan Rivers says, "A bracelet announces, 'This is where the cloth ends and the flesh begins. To me, there is something unfinished about an outfit that doesn't include a bracelet."

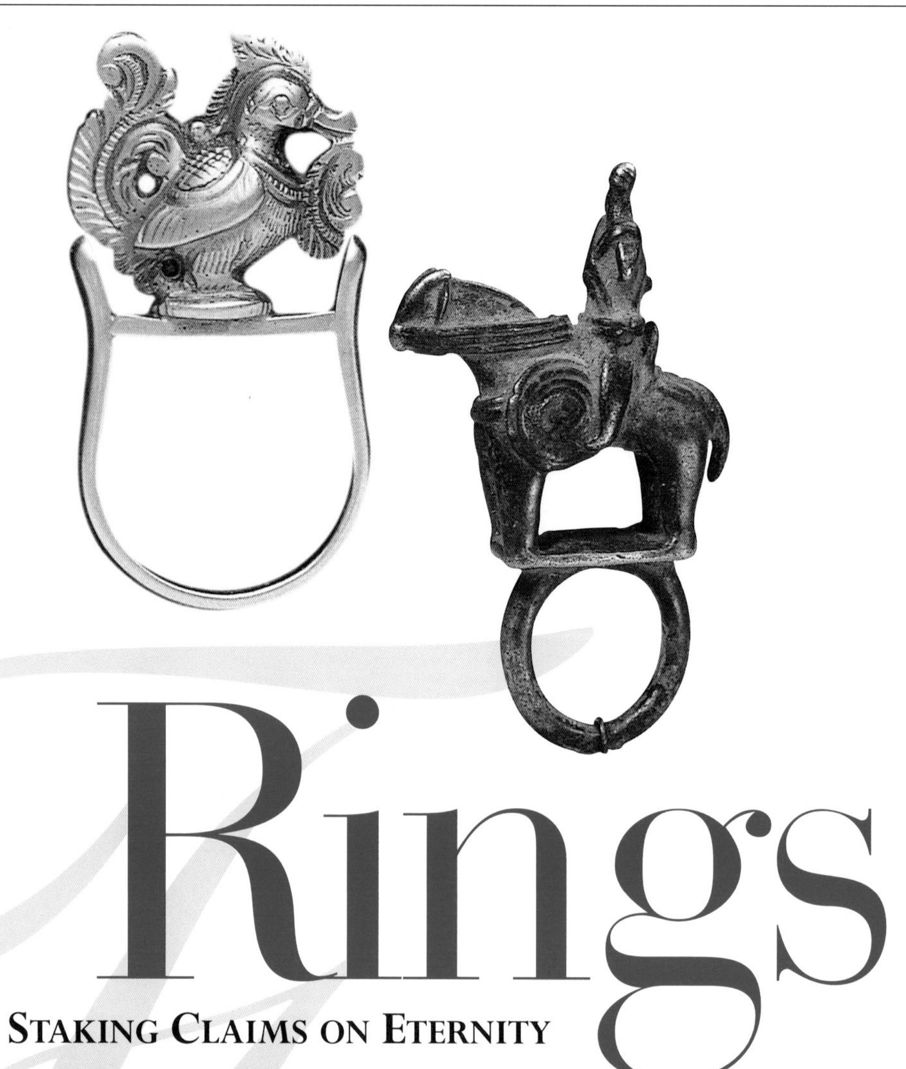

Rings

Staking Claims on Eternity

For all its dignity as it sits quietly on a finger, modest in size compared to the average necklace or brooch, the ring is jewelry's most revealing piece. Upon noticing a ring, one begins to ponder: Is he married? Is her fiancée wealthy? What school did he attend? One glance at the ring finger of a bejeweled hand can yield information worth its weight in gold.

ABOVE LEFT
Gold ring with white goose, considered a vehicle of Brahma, god of Creation.

ABOVE RIGHT
Ring featuring a soldier on a horse, representing the captain of the Legion.

FACING PAGE
African princess wears a pure gold ring that represents power, fertility and health.

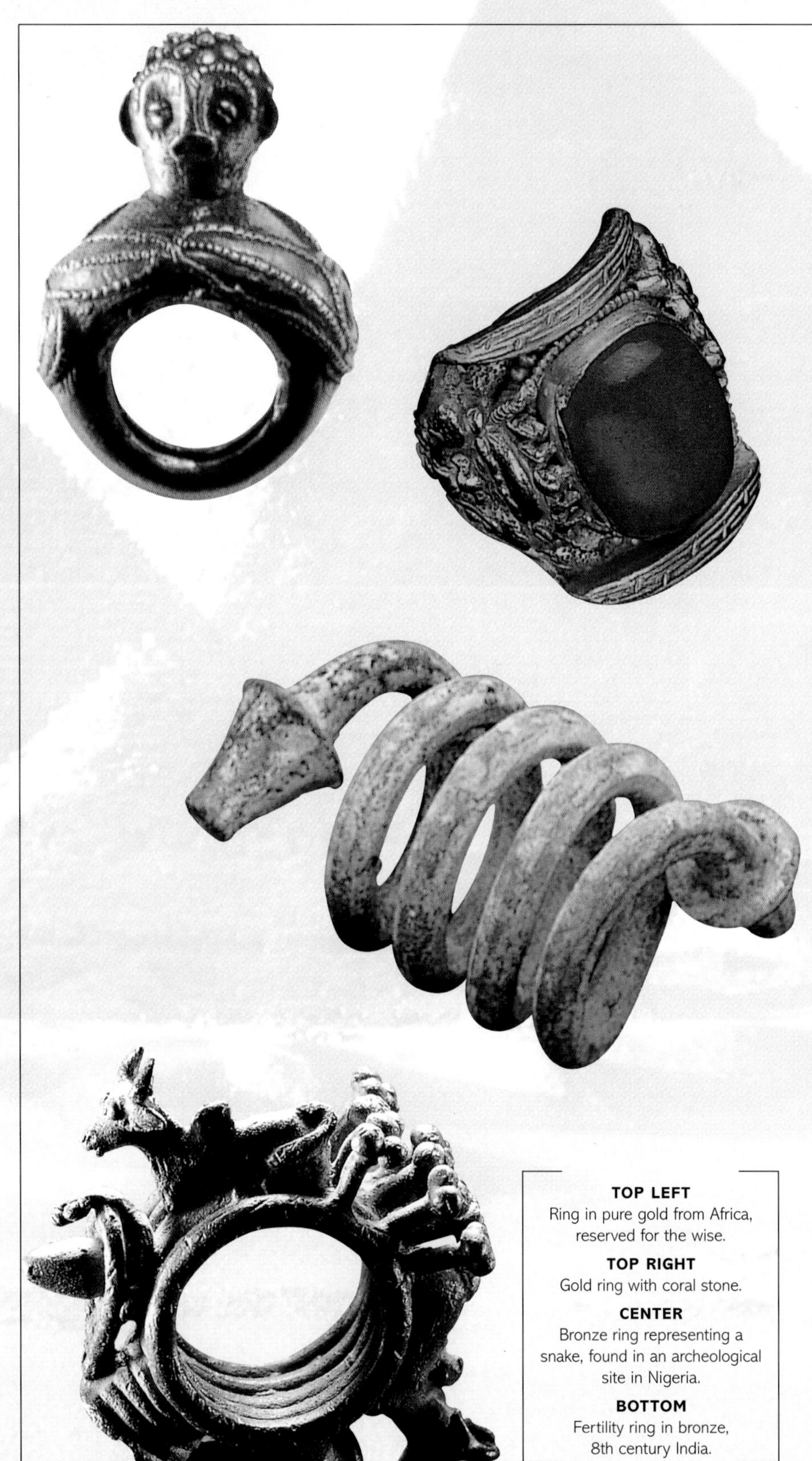

TOP LEFT
Ring in pure gold from Africa, reserved for the wise.
TOP RIGHT
Gold ring with coral stone.
CENTER
Bronze ring representing a snake, found in an archeological site in Nigeria.
BOTTOM
Fertility ring in bronze, 8th century India.

In ancient times, the significance of the ring was often quite different for each sex. On a woman, rings were primarily decorative; for a man, rings signified power. According to the Bible, when Pharaoh designated Joseph ruler of Egypt, he "took off his ring from his hand and put it on Joseph's hand." During the Roman Empire, one measure of a man's success and professional status was the number of rings on his fingers. Women, on the other hand, wore rings to enhance their beauty. Rings rich in symbolism — of power, love, status — also served more practical purposes.

Many styles of finger-rings — archer's thumb-rings; marriage, betrothal and love rings; mourning and commemorative rings — were designed for functional use and special occassions. In some instances it is purely by chance that these rings turned out to be exceptionally beautiful as well.

By the 16th century, wealthy men and women alike often wore great quantities of rings. The fingers of Henry VIII, a Venetian ambassador noted, were "one mass of jeweled rings." And by 1600, the great age of the goldsmith was over and the stone setter had become the star. Rings, set with precious and semiprecious stones, reflected this trend.

During the 18th century, stones looked more beautiful than ever because of improvements made in faceting and foiling. Dazzling from beneath long lace sleeves, rings were the ultimate glamour accessory. Madame de

Pompadour (1721-64), who set the standard of taste and fashion for her generation, had a collection of over forty rings. However, her lover Louis XV did not share her affection for rings. Thus, she put them on as soon as he left her company and removed them when he came back.

ABOVE
A cavalier on a camel, in bronze. Found in a tomb in Egypt.
RIGHT
Ring belonging to an oracle or psychic. Roosters were a common ritual sacrifice.

Grandiosity in rings reappeared during the 19th century. Rings were so huge, in fact, that men complained they could not kiss the hand of a lady without being bruised by her jewels. By the last half of the century, the great houses of jewelry — Cartier and Fouquet, most notably — were creating stunning works of art. Diamonds, formerly set in silver to set off their whiteness were now being showcased in the more pristine platinum.

The 20th century boasts ring designs that run the full gamut. At the Exposition Universelle of 1990, Rene Lalique showcased naturalistic designs spun from gold and enamel and highlighted with a mere sprinkling of diamonds. George Fouquet, in collaboration with the artist Alphonse Mucha, created a spectacular snake bracelet with ring for the actress Sarah Bernhardt, whose fingers were never without a menagerie of rings.

ABOVE
The Sphinx, Egypt.
RIGHT
Bronze rings from Mali.
BELOW
Gold ring whose size indicates the power of the wearer. Ghana.

ABOVE
Ring in gold, set with seven rubies. 17th century.

FAR LEFT
Painting by Horace Vernet. 1819, Cairo.

LEFT
Two views of a men's ring, enameled polychrome with diamond set in gold.

The larger-than-life rings of the Art Deco period often featured huge geometrical designs. Cartier created the Trinity ring, consisting of three hoops of red, yellow and white gold, fitting and twisting neatly into each other. Van Cleef & Arpels created the invisible setting, in which stones are massed into a mosaic of pure color secured by wires hidden on the back of the ring. And as each era came and went, leaving behind a legacy of jewelry designs, one thing remained constant: the desire to transform one's fingers into displays of wealth, status and beauty.

FAR LEFT
Scene of Women at the Fountain, Auxere Musée de Beaux Art.

LEFT
Thumb ring engraved in gold with rubies, sapphires and diamonds.

BELOW
Byzantine-style rings in 18K gold. Lalaounis.

Signet rings played an important role before literacy became widespread. Essential for government and commerce, the signet ring bore a distinguishing mark or badge that could be impressed on clay or wax to authenticate correspondence, documents and seals on property.

Early signets sometimes were engraved with a portrait. Julius Caesar, who claimed he was a descendent of the goddess Venus, wore a ring with her image. Other emperors reigned with more vanity, wearing signets bearing their own portraits. The portrait signet was subsequently revived at the end of the medieval period and continued to be a popular accessory well into the 19th century.

To illustrate some of the more ethereal qualities associated with the ring, the poet Ovid waxed sentimental over the signet he bestowed upon his beloved: "May she receive thee with glad heart and straightway slip thee on her finger; mayst thou fit her as well as she fits me, and press her finger with aptly adjusted circle!... To help her seal her secret missives, and to keep the dry, clinging gem from drawing away the wax, I should first touch the moist lips of my beautiful love." The signet to which Ovid refers was graced by the visage of Cupid.

There is a long history behind the archer's thumb-ring, which was primarily a functional ring, but often very decorative as well. A 5th-century Chinese ring of brownish-green jade dates from the period when the crossbow was created. An Indian ring from the 17th century is fashioned from gray-green jade, inlaid with rubies and emeralds and set with gold. A 14th-century Venetian archer's thumb ring doubled as a charm to protect the wearer from the dangers of

TOP
Shiva and Parvati, India, 12th century.

CENTER
Three-unit silver toe-ring set ornamented with bunches of small balls resembling fish roe, a fertility symbol.

LOWER LEFT
Silver dorsal hand ornament that includes, in addition to the usual elements, ornaments for the finger ends. Ahmadabad, Gujarat.

LOWER RIGHT
Two views of white-nephrite hololithic thumb ring inlaid with rubies and emeralds set in gold. North India, 18th century.

TOP LEFT
Portrait of Napoleon by David. The Louvre.

TOP RIGHT
Ring set with a diamond engraved with a French baron's coronet, surrounded by calibré-cut sapphires. Mounted in gold by Pelletier in 1900. Boucheron.

travel.

The fede, or hand-in-hand, ring first made its appearance in Roman times, when the two clasped hands represented a contract. Rings play an important part in the marriage rituals of early Christian times. The ring, given by the man to the woman, was a symbol of mutual fidelity. It was placed on the fourth finger because a certain vein is said to flow from that point straight to the heart.

Jewish weddings rings have traditionally had the Hebrew phrase *Mazal Tov* (Good Luck) inscribed on the roof of a small building designed atop the bezel. This building represents both the Temple of Jerusalem and the home in which the couple will live together, harkening back to the Talmudic phrase, "his house is his wife."

ABOVE
Presentation ring given by Napoleon to the Commander of the Horse Guard at Nimeguen in Holland. This ring bears the crowned cipher "N". Other presentation rings bore the eagle. Gold, rose and brilliant-cut diamonds.

FAR LEFT
Louis XV at Versaille.

LEFT
Gem engraving was one of Madame de Pompadour's chief interests; taught by Jacques Guay, she succeeded in carving a cameo portrait of her lover, Louis XV.

RIGHT
An early 15th-century gold ring from Chalcis, set with an ancient amethyst intaglio of Abundantia holding her cornucopia. The inscription on the hoop is in Lombardic letters and translates as, "The Word was made flesh," a Biblical phrase believed to avert seizures.

In the 18th century, rings given as love tokens were light and graceful. Locks of hair were often set in rings to console lovers forced to be apart from one another. Marie-Joseph de Saxe, the daughter-in-law of Louis XV, wore a ring with the hair of her hus-

CLOCKWISE FROM ABOVE

Gold ring with a royal coat of arms.

Gold archer's thumb ring with six Mughal-cut diamonds, twenty-one flat and cabochon rubies and fourteen emeralds, all foil-backed and mounted kundun-style. Delhi, 1625-50.

Louis XVI wearing a ring on his leg with a large diamond centerpiece — later named "l'ordre de la jaretiere" by the Queen of England.

After the death of Napoleon at St. Helena in 1821, the admirals wore this ring (shown in two views) to commemorate him. The side opens to reveal a picture of the emperor.

Ecclesiastical ring worn by priests, with the engraving of an angel in amber, set in gold.

band, the Dauphin, identified by a diamond cipher.

Portrait rings, depicting a man and a woman facing each other in profile, were also popular. A cameo ring of the future Louis XVI of France and his bride Marie-Antoinette commemorates their marriage. In 1840, Queen Victoria and Prince Albert also chose portrait rings to celebrate their marriage. In early Tudor times, however, newlyweds began to opt for the less-is-more variety. A simple gold loop, such as the one given by Phillip II of Spain to Mary I of England, is still the most common wedding ring today.

The posy ring, a gold hoop decorated with trails of running foliage, was inscribed with a short verse, or "posy," from such tomes as *The Mysteries of Love* or *The Arts of Wooing*, or composed especially for the couple. These rings were constant reminders to the couple to "keep faith till death" and to never forget that their hearts were "joined in God" — and "what God has joined together..."

The 20th century has seen marriages — and marriage tokens — of unprecedented wealth and ostentation. Barbara Hutton, for her engagement to a European prince in 1933, chose a black pearl from Cartier. Designer Paul Flato won a reputation among the Hollywood set for his

diamond solitaires. His clients included Clare Booth Luce. Wallis Simpson selected rings to symbolize not only weddings, but divorce as well. Cartier was her designer of choice. The Duchess of Kent, for her wedding, made a patriotic statement: she chose three eternity rings, one each of rubies, diamonds and sapphires, representing the British flag.

More recently Barbra Streisand traded in her 10-carat diamond engagement ring from James Brolin for a smaller version she could comfortably wear every day. Sotheby's auctioned off the 40-carat diamond ring given by Aristotle Onassis to Jackie Kennedy Onassis in 1968 for $2.6 million. And tragically, Prince William now owns the sapphire and diamond engagement ring his father, Prince Charles, gave to his mother, Princess Diana.

Upon the death of a monarch, it was common to wear a commemo-

TOP LEFT
The Kiss by Gustave Klimt.

TOP RIGHT
Two women dancing with scarves from the Art Nouveau Epoque.

CENTER LEFT
The restaurant Maxim's in Paris.

CENTER RIGHT
Diamond ring in platinum by Martin Gruber.

BOTTOM LEFT
The famous beauty, La Belle Otero — mistress of kings, "demi-mondaine".

BOTTOM RIGHT
Ring with diamonds, rubies and pearls set in gold. Mauboussin.

rative ring bearing the monarch's portrait. The most notorious example is the ring made to commemorate Charles I. Under a hinged gold enameled cover was a portrait of the Emperor Napoleon, said to be one of six made for the conspirators involved in the escape of Napoleon from the Isle of Elba. During the 14th century, portrait rings of deceased relatives and friends served as *mementi mori*.

To ensure good luck, wolves' teeth were set in pairs for engagement rings. The Archbishop Tension, Duke of Monmouth (1649-85), believed a charm laid under the stone in his ring would save him from danger and defeat in battle. His belief, unfortunately, was unsubstantiated, as is true of the many magical properties ascribed to rings. This has done little to detract from the popularity of such beliefs, however. Philip II of Spain wore a ring set with a stone to prevent hemorrhages; Queen Elizabeth wore a ring to protect from illness. Cramp rings fashioned from silver and gold were hugely popular in Scotland, where they were worn as charms against epilepsy, convulsions and other spasmodic disorders. A 14th-century medical treatise described how they were to be manufactured: while prayers were recited, they were to be inscribed with the names of two of the Magi and a magic phrase.

TOP LEFT
Crystal diamonds with a row of onyx mounted in platinum. This style became popular in 1927.

TOP RIGHT
Claudette Colbert wearing an art deco ring in crystal and diamonds.

BOTTOM LEFT
Design for a step-cut sapphire, mounted in platinum and set with baguette-cut diamonds. Boucheron, 1937.

BOTTOM CENTER
Art deco ring, sapphire and diamonds set in gold. Boucheron, 1940.

BOTTOM RIGHT
Carved jade in platinum. Boucheron, 1930.

TOP LEFT
Painting of a Jewish wedding.

TOP RIGHT
Happy Diamonds collection. Rings in 18K white gold, with one free-moving diamond. Chopard.

BOTTOM LEFT
18K yellow gold "lacet" ring with approximately 56 pavé diamonds. Alexandre Reza.

BOTTOM RIGHT
"Axelle" rings in precious stones and diamonds in platinum. Boucheron.

Before its role as centerpiece of the classic engagement ring was established, the diamond served as a diplomatic gift. Rubies, synonymous with luxury, were at one time more highly valued than diamonds. The sapphire stood for hope, the topaz for duty, the garnet for love and the emerald for faith. Pearls symbolized purity, virtue. An amethyst was thought to keep the wearer sober.

Cameos, precious and semiprecious stones on which a design has been carved in relief, have also been highly prized for use in rings. Early examples of man's passion for cameos come from ancient Sumeria (c. 2000 BC). Medusa is the most common design on Roman Britain cameos. Henry VIII wore a cameo ring set with a child's head, perhaps a representation of the son he coveted. A French cameo depicts the head of Mme de Maintenon (1635-1719) who was secretly married to Louis XIV in 1684.

The "Fisherman's Ring," which

TOP

(Left) Gianni Versace ring in gold setting with d-flawless diamonds. (Center) A de Grisogono ring set with 17 carats of natural black diamonds and a pearl of 16.5mm. (Right) Ring with a spectacular emerald and diamonds. Alexandre Reza.

CENTER

(Left)A sapphire enhanced by baguette- and square-cut diamonds, forming a fleur-de-lis and butterflies. Chaumet. (Center)Diamonds and yellow gold. Boucheron. (Right) Ring in gold with a ruby and diamonds. Chanel.

BOTTOM

(Left) Rings in 18K white or yellow gold, each set with 134 diamonds and 20 trapeze-cut sapphires, rubies or diamonds. Chopard. (Center) Two rings from the *Pietra Dura* collection by Piranesi. (Right) Burmese sapphire and diamond ring in gold.

TOP
"Sonia" consists of a fine brand of "square" diamonds flanked by two wider bands generously set with diamonds. Boucheron.

UPPER LEFT
Diamond ring in gold with d-flawless diamond. Gianni Versace.

FAR LEFT
Comet diamond ring set in gold. Chanel.

CENTER
Pink heart diamond. Chopard.

BOTTOM
Three gold rings set with colored precious stones. Verdura.

FACING PAGE
"Anneau" rings, in yellow gold inlaid with white or yellow pavé diamonds. Chaumet.

has become the investiture ring of the popes, is first referred to in a letter from Clement IV to his nephew in 1265. Victorian collectors gave the name "Papal" to a group of enormous gilt-metal rings set with paste and bearing the coats-of-arms of popes from Marin V (1416-31) to Innocent VIII (1484-91) as well as those of a few cardinals, bishops and secular princes. The earliest mention of a ring given as a papal gift to a newly appointed cardinal is in 1294. Cardinal Pietro Barbo, years before becoming pope, owned an impressive set of rings to wear over his liturgical gloves when celebrating High Mass. Several were set with huge, table-cut sapphires.

Catholic nuns, beginning in the 11th century, wore plain gold bands inscribed "This is the ring of chastity/I am the spouse of Jesus Christ." English widows who took vows of perpetual chastity wore similar rings. When captured by the English in 1430, Joan of Arc was wearing a latten ring inscribed with the names of Jesus and Mary. Such rings, bearing the names of saints, Biblical quotations and monograms, prospered during that time. The letter "M" stood for the Virgin Mary. The letters "IHS" express a desire for Christ's protection.

Today's rings are no less status symbols than those of yesteryear. A class rings boasts of a prized education. Athletic championship rings are the ultimate symbols of sports achievement. A man is today encouraged — even expected — to spend as much as possible, two months' salary at the least, on an engagement ring for his beloved. A mere glance at the ring finger of most any hand can reveal much.

Objects

Treasures Kept at Hand

VERDURA'S SEASHELL COMPACT adorned with cabochon sapphires, Boucheron's ornate mother-of-pearl cigarette box and Van Cleef & Arpels' much-coveted Minaudière clutch — all are ornately adorned to provide the owner with the ultimate in luxury. Beautiful jeweled objects can bring joy to everyday tasks: writing a letter, scenting oneself with perfume, applying make-up or lighting a cigarette. They make the perfect gift for the person who possesses every other item of jewelry imaginable. And because they are not worn as fashion accessories like other jewelry, jeweled objects are perhaps more strongly associated with the memory of the giver. Gilded in precious gold, adorned with dazzling gemstones, these objects convey a particular sense of the timeless, of the eternal.

LEFT
Miniature carriage made in vermeil and precious stones, a replica of an actual carriage created for the wedding of Louis II of Bauiere and the Duchess Sophia.

FACING PAGE
Versailles

The snuffbox, for one, played an important role in rituals establishing trust between two strangers. During social occasions, it was customary to offer a pinch from one's snuffbox after first publicly sampling it oneself. This gesture ensured that the contents were not poisonous and also provided an easy means of breaking the ice. Snuffboxes quickly drew the attention of artists, who crafted them in unusual shapes and ornate styles, enhancing their appeal.

The concept of stowing treasures within adorned vessels traces back to the ancient funerary customs of the Sumerians and Egyptians, who were buried with their finest jewelry pieces so as to be properly adorned in the hereafter. The ancients collected jewelry and endowed their ornaments with tremendous significance. Pearls represented purity, rubies strength, garnets devotion and amethysts were believed to keep one sober. Jade was, and still is, sought after in China for its ability to protect its wearer from harm while also bringing good fortune.

The adornment of everyday objects became widespread during the Roman and Greek Empires.

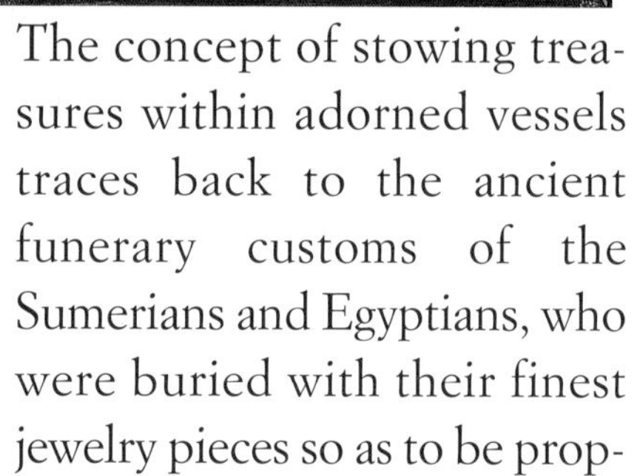

Perhaps the most fanciful objects ever to be adorned are the world-famous eggs crafted by Carl Fabergé. Intricately festooned, the small and ornate items were considered by their creator to be worth more than their weight in gold. "The value of the work is ten times the value of the material," was the philosophy of Carl Fabergé. In 1870, at the tender age of twenty-four, Carl took over his ailing father's jewelry firm. At this time, he was already famous for his egg designs.

TOP LEFT
The journey of the Emperor of China tapestry made by Royale of Beauvais.

TOP CENTER
Men's lighter made in bronze. The fish symbolizes tenacity.

TOP RIGHT
Buckle made in gold with diamonds, sapphires, and rubies. Boucheron.

CENTER LEFT
"Intro" from Japan, 18th century, lacquered box with mother-of-pearl fish.

LEFT
Netsuke, 1800, made in ivory. Painted by Dyded.

FAR LEFT
Netsuke, 1800, made in ivory.

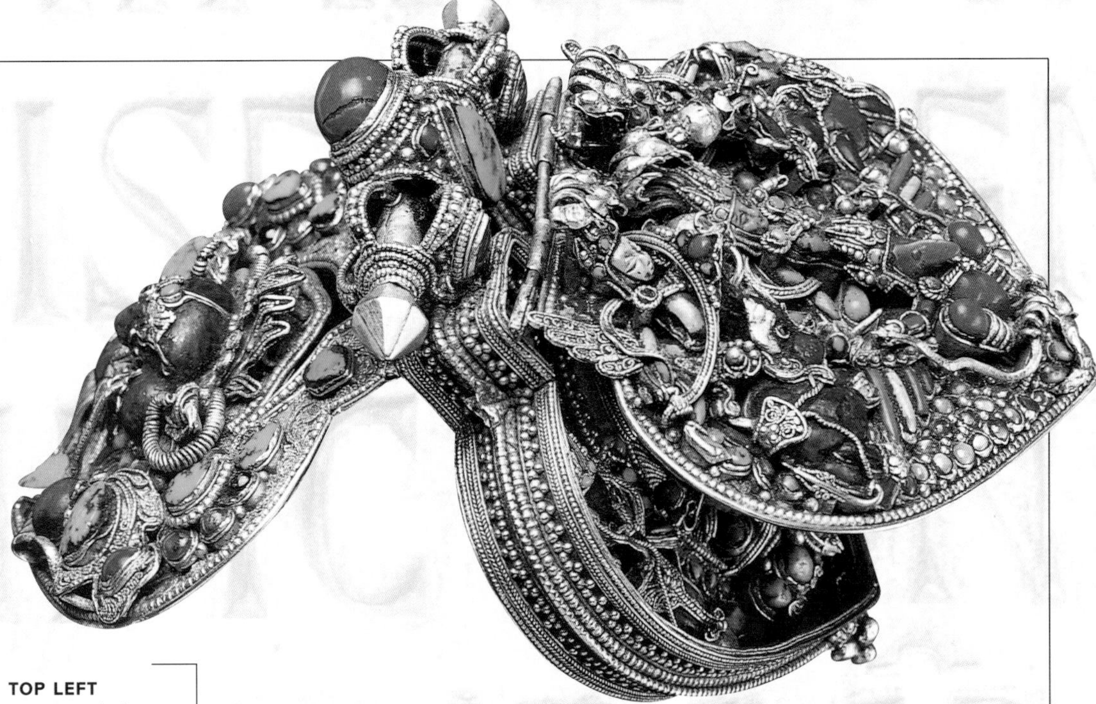

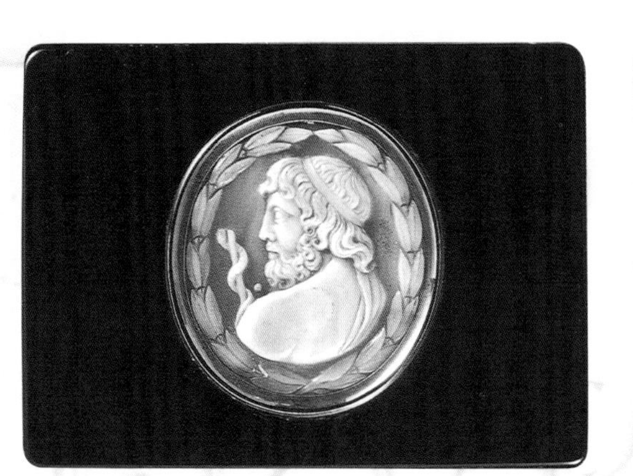

TOP LEFT
Ivory box composed of two carved heart-shaped compartments, with a chased gold mount. c. 1900. Boucheron collection.

TOP RIGHT
Pillbox in gold made of lapis-lazuli, coral emeralds, garnet, pearls and semiprecious stones.

CENTER LEFT
Snuffbox with Cipher of the Empress Marie-Louise made in gold, silver, enamel and rose diamonds. The rose diamond cipher of the Empress is set against an engine-turned ground enamelled blue, within a chased border of acanthus scrolls, palmettes and rosettes. Chaumet.

CENTER RIGHT
Snuffbox with Napoleon's Cipher made in gold, silver, enamel, and oblong diamonds. The diamond cipher N for Napoleon is set within a border enamelled blue with trails of leaves in chased gold. Chaumet.

BOTTOM LEFT
Snuffbox with Cameo of Aesculapius made in gold tortoiseshell and agate cameo. Aesculapius, god of healing, holds his serpentine staff. Chaumet.

BOTTOM RIGHT
Snuffbox with Augustus and Livia Cameo made in gold, blue enamel border and cameo. Chaumet.

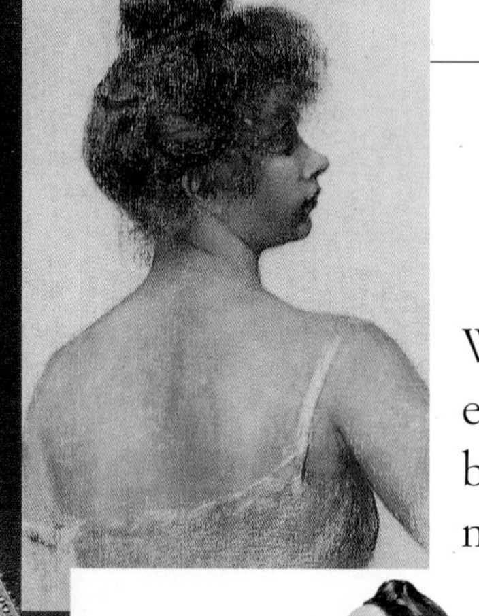

With increasing wealth and more modern means of transportation, travel became more common during the nineteenth century. The well-heeled traveler required a complete set of grooming accessories and writing implements. Ornate sets might included matching lighters, lorgnettes, hair and nail trimmers and an inkwell and pen. To complete the set, and ensure correspondence remained private, many travelers carried a wax stamp with which to seal envelopes.

Fabergé produced his first celebratory Easter egg for Russia's imperial family in 1885, and each Easter thereafter surprised the Romanovs with his inventiveness. Each egg contained a surprise within: a golden coach, for example, or a small, bejeweled crown. Nicholas II presented a mosaic egg to the Tsarina, Alexandra Feodorovna, on Easter morning in 1914.

Fashion demands of the same period posed certain problems for women, particularly the tightly drawn corsets, which caused some to faint. A beautiful, high-jeweled scent bottle, waved under the delicate nostrils, would awaken the distressed maiden. In order to preempt the problem, women also carried fans encrusted with jewels, or painted with refined images, to wave under their overheated visages.

ABOVE LEFT
Clockwise, from 18th century, desk accessories made in gold, crystal, lapis lazuli, and semi-precious stones. Necessities for traveling made in gold with turquoise. Glasses case made in gold engraving. Lighter made in gold and mother-of-pearl.

TOP CENTER
The Dancer by Pierre Carrier Belleure, 1900.

ABOVE CENTER
A dandy from the Belle Époque.

CENTER
A fan reproduced from *The Fur and The Fance*, 1911.

FAR LEFT
Elephant clock by J. B. Moisy.

BELOW LEFT
Cigarette case with mother-of-pearl panels set into green and yellow gold repoussé borders, engraved in Louis XVI style. The lid is decorated with a floret centring on a diamond within an oval frame. The thumb-push is set with a navette diamond. Boucheron collection

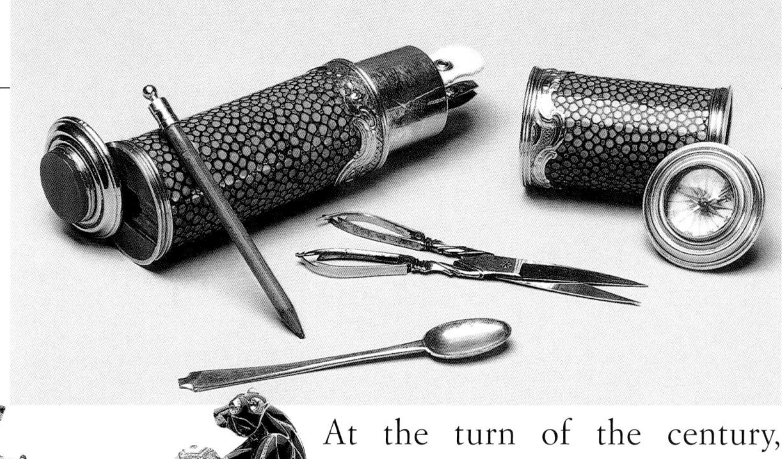

At the turn of the century, Frédéric Boucheron created numerous items for members of royalty, high society and luminaries, including ivory pin boxes, rock crystal scent bottles and tiepins, a diamond-studded version of which was snapped up by Oscar Wilde. Under the powerful vision of Boucheron, ordinary, functional items were transformed into luxurious objets d'art.

TOP
18th century objects made in gold and galluchat.

ABOVE
Clock made in gold, diamonds, rubies, and mother of pearl with two mechanical bears. Mauboussin.

FAR RIGHT
Advertisement from the Samaritan department store in Paris.

CENTER
Snuffbox made in gold, accented with different colors of semiprecious stones.

BOTTOM
Vanity case with chinese-style decorations, made in nephrite, lapis lazuli and diamonds. Chaumet, 1925.

BOTTOM RIGHT
Clamshell compact, in gold, adorned with diamonds and sapphires. Verdura.

Jeweled objects would reach a new level of elegance and refinement during the art deco period as a variety of accessories were elevated to starring roles. Card boxes and cigarette and powder cases were enshrined in sapphires and diamonds, onyx and enamel. Since mirrors were not so common during this era, women who wanted to wear make-up relied heavily on their compacts and vanity cases. Mary Pickford's gold and black enamel vanity case, created by Cartier, contained a powder compartment and a small tube of lipstick that had to be returned to the jeweler to be refilled.

Cigarette holders — sensationally sculpted — made smoking seem elegant. In the speakeasies, cigarette-smoking flappers flashed their bejeweled lighters. On film screens, glamorous stars inhaled deeply through burnished cigarette holders fashioned with diamonds, white onyx and black lacquer. Another hallmark art deco item was a toilet case created by Chaumet in gold and black enamel, adorned in a floral motif featuring coral, lapis lazuli and diamonds.

As these beautiful objects overflowed the purses of the wealthy and the stylish, the purse itself became a new area of experimentation for jewelry designers. Mauboussin designed an evening bag that featured engraved emeralds bordered by red enamel, brilliants and a circular medallion on the clasp. The handle was enhanced with ribbed emerald beads, red enamel and brilliants on a platinum mount. Van Cleef & Arpels invented the unique Minaudière evening bag. Sleek and shiny, the boxy gold clutch was adorned with gems — inside of which a woman could toss her lipstick, cigarettes, comb or jewels. The Arpels brothers named the clutch for their sister, Estelle, who they had nicknamed Minaudière, meaning simper, a skill she exercised with unrivaled charm.

When actress Jean Harlow smoked a cigarette with intent to seduce in the film *Public Enemy*, it was from a dia-

FAR LEFT
Mademoiselle Damy, 1905. Her hat, by Crozet, is kept in place by a long pin, and there are combs in her upswept hair. Chaumet.

TOP CENTER
Engraved rock-crystal smelling-salt bottle, the stopper set with a cushion-shaped amethyst and diamonds. 1890-1900. Private collection.

TOP RIGHT
Hair ornaments, the tines of blond tortoise-shell, the gold openwork heads decorated with "centered on a pearl" enamel, set with rose diamonds. Boucheron, 1870.

ABOVE
Circular carved bonbonnière. The lid decorated with a woman wearing a garland of mistletoe and with a gold sickle symbolizing the harvest. Boucheron.

BOTTOM RIGHT
Seal of the Marquise de Blocqueville is made of gold, agate and lapis lazuli. Chaumet.

CENTER
Love Trophy combs made for a wedding present. The ribbons frame a trophy comprising two symbols of love, Cupid's quiver and a flaming torch. Chaumet.

BOTTOM LEFT
The Dog Rose, the most common of European wild roses, in 18K gold. Lalaounis.

ABOVE
Cufflinks set in gold. Verdura.

RIGHT
Photo by Irving Penn. Spring/Summer Collection 1992. Gianni Versace.

BOTTOM RIGHT
Pill box made in pure gold.

BELOW
Black Diamonds collection portable phone. de Grisogono.

mond and black onyx cigarette holder by Cartier. And when Scarlett O'Hara launched a new fashion trend when she wore a graceful snood in *Gone with the Wind*, many women followed suit, fastening their hair into nets adorned with ribbons, pearls or velvet.

In 1968, the same year that Cartier launched its first collection of 18-karat gold watches, the designer also introduced its instantly popular and now-famous oval cigarette lighter. A few years later the Les Must de Cartier line was christened, bringing leather goods, pens, perfumes and glasses new status. A contemporary devotee of Cartier design is singer/songwriter Elton John. His prized jewelry collection includes Les Must de Cartier sunglasses as well as diamond and platinum brooches.

Today's fast-paced lifestyles have spawned new objects to adorn. The modern era of communications has given us the cellular phone, the personal pager and the laptop computer, adding to the many other useful devices of daily living that provide a tableaux for the expression of the jewelers' imaginations.

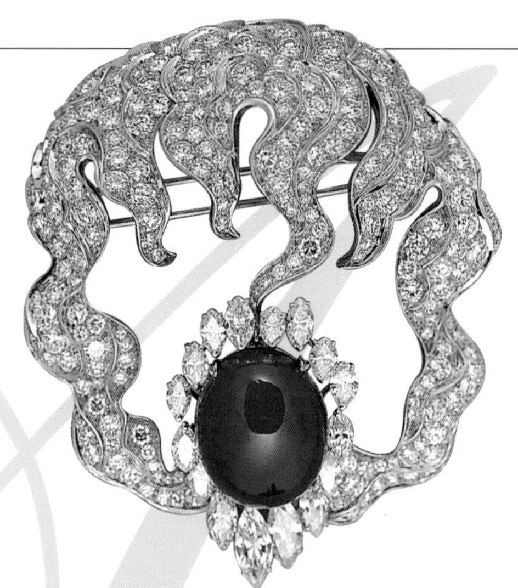

ALEXANDRE REZA EXEMPLIFIES THE BONDS FORGED between man and stones. He knows them, certainly, but he can imagine them because he speaks directly to them. Body and soul, his entire existence has been devoted to this dialogue, which in the course of the years has become a quasi-magical duet. His jewels are the reflection of a conversation that begins with gems in the rough and culminates in perfection.

ABOVE
Sapphire and diamond brooch.
BELOW
Sapphire and diamond earrings.
FACING PAGE
Parure of sapphires and diamonds.

Alexandre Reza

Born in Moscow, Alexandre Reza came to France as a child. He kept the gentle sparkle of Samarkand where his mother was born and the pomp and mysteries of his father who was a goldsmith from Moscow. He grew up in the south and the urge to dedicate his life to stones never left him.

However, circumstances were hardly auspicious and France would see bad times. Perhaps it was then that Alexandre Reza learned patience and caution in daily life, which did not prevent him from experiencing the camp of Drancy and the British camp of Saint-Denis. His hopes dashed but strengthened by a long period of forced immobility, after the Liberation he finally began to live his life as he had imagined it.

His knowledge of stones is innate and was not gained through books. He goes to the sources and examines the thousands of carats, scrutinizes the ancients and listens to their silences, because often these men who speak to stones are parsimonious with words. But their gestures tell more than words. And he lends an attentive ear to the echo the gems inspire in him, as if to help him come to know them better.

This tête-à-tête allows him to cultivate flawless judgement of stones, even those that look imperfect to the untrained eye. A carving well done can erase imperfections and can give the stone density and uniformity. An art few jewelers can master, it requires the ability to apprehend at first glance a stone's possibilities unaided by anything save intuition and a keen eye.

Quick appreciation is essential to surpass the visible to get to the

COUNTERCLOCKWISE FROM TOP
Necklace of emerald hearts and diamonds. Empress Farah Pahlavi of Iran with Alexandre Reza. Prince Rainier of Monaco in Alexandre Reza's store in Monaco. Sapphire and diamond brooch. Sapphire and diamond pendant earrings. Sapphire and diamond ring.

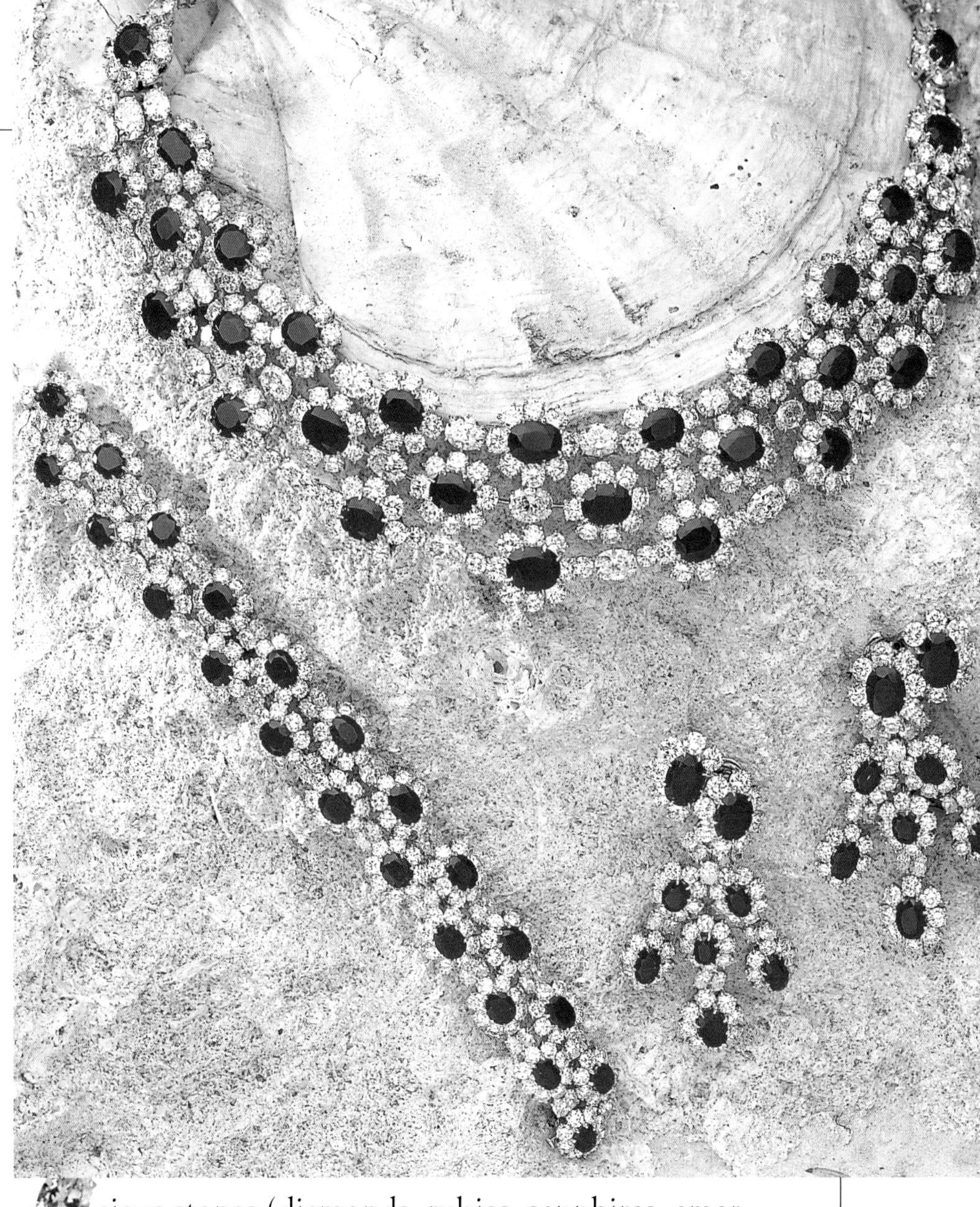

hidden truth. It is the result of arduous labor and relentless will, and it strives for unattainable but always inspiring perfection. A creator by instinct, Alexandre Reza assembles exceptional stones around one object. One-of-a-kind beauty is multiplied and becomes a work of art where each element is at once the soloist and orchestra, setting off and enhancing each surrounding piece.

The reconstitution of ancient jewels has been the life's work of Alexandre Reza. Taking his cue from old drawings, he rescues a classic jewel from oblivion and brings it back to life with his colors and imagination, which are the reflection of his age. He is the sleeping beauty that wakes up to our century and deploys the grace and charms of his time.

The jewel was born with man. Ornament, talisman, sign of belonging to a man or a clan, or a bit of everything, the jewel has remained his faithful companion throughout the ages. The notion of jewelry is linked to the use of precious stones (diamonds, rubies, sapphires, emeralds) and is a relatively modern concept.

Working from the drawings of the great painters of the Renaissance like Holbein, Alexandre Reza has uncovered a veritable challenge by effacing himself before the author as he gives him full expression through his splendid stones. And it is a genuine success.

ABOVE LEFT
Heart-shaped emerald and diamond ring.

ABOVE CENTER
Pear-shaped emerald and diamond pendant earrings.

ABOVE
On three rows spangled with diamonds, 74 rubies weave a sumptuous lattice from which emanates all the mystery of Burma.

LEFT
Diamond necklace with a pear-shaped diamond pendant.

At ease with Gilles Legar, engraver and goldsmith to Louis XIV, Montcornet and Morisson, great masters in a dynasty of jewelers from beyond the Rhine, he is also receptive to the delicate meanderings of the rococco. Paintings like Rouget's of the marriage of Napoleon and Marie-Louise of Austria have also inspired Alexandre Reza. The rare sumptuousness of Rouget's canvas is summed up in the reconstruction of the necklace worn by Caroline Bonaparte, sister of the emperor who attented the ceremony in the cortege of the maids of honor. And, closer to us, the cartoons of Bapst and Julienne provide him with sources in Romanticism and the Second Empire.

ABOVE
Diamond and ruby necklace with 3 pear-shape DI flawless light pink I flawless intense blue I flawless.

LEFT
"Trembleuse" parure with Birmans rubies.

BELOW
Ruby and diamond bracelet.

Over many centuries, under different guises, the jewel is always seductive and precious and has evolved with the whims of political and economic life in France. The jewel was the prestigious and costly symbol of the French nobility that the clairvoyant Louis XIV had gathered around him in Versailles. The Revolution concealed it, carrier of withering ambitions and lost hope. And then it reemerged, leaving behind some of its price but none of its grace and let the newly born bourgeoisie taste its charms — without lèse-majesté.

The contemporary jewels of Alexandre Reza

ABOVE
Twenty-seven lozenge and square-cut emeralds offer themselves in a setting of circular-cut diamonds to create the necklace of this striking parure.

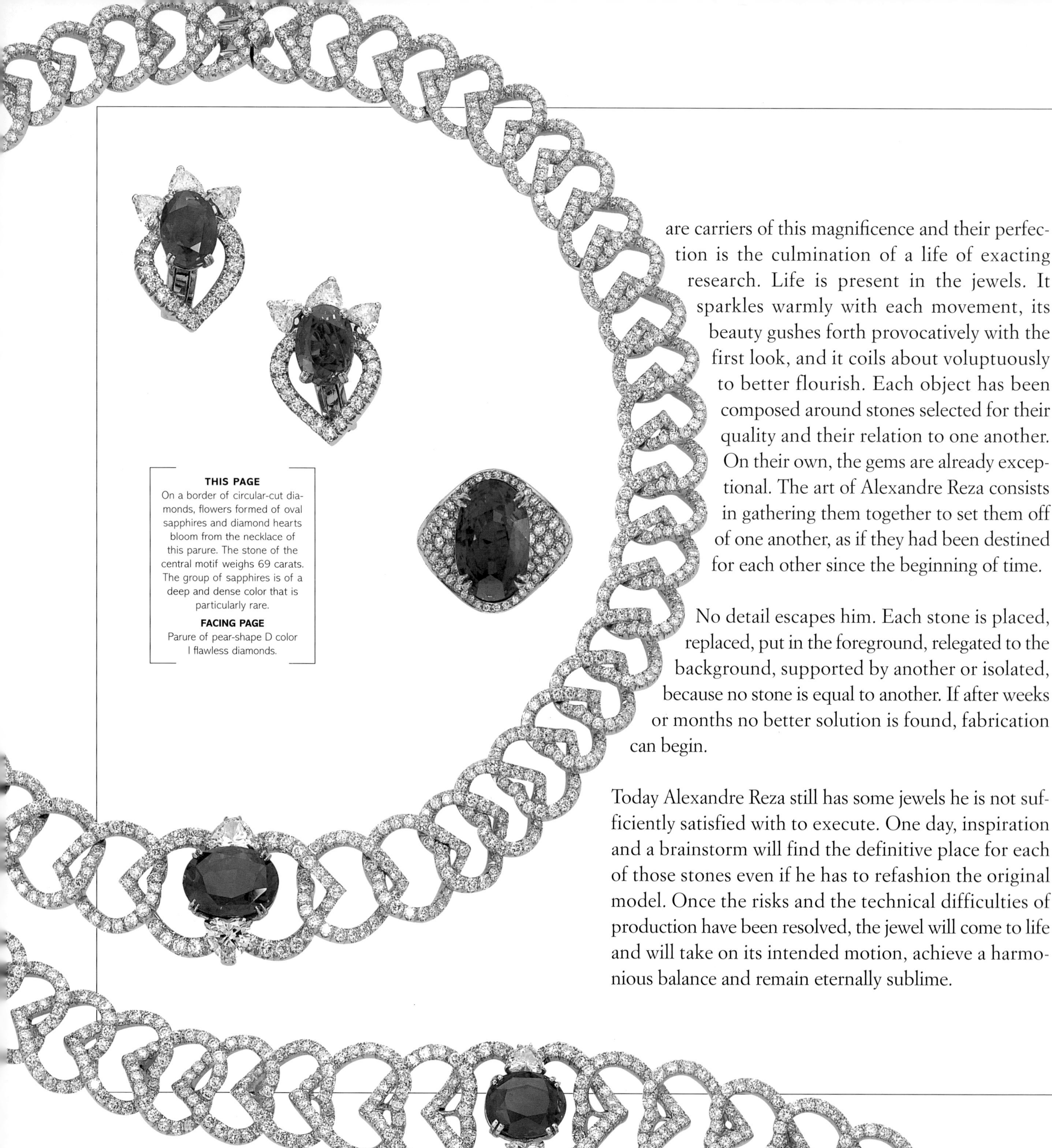

THIS PAGE
On a border of circular-cut diamonds, flowers formed of oval sapphires and diamond hearts bloom from the necklace of this parure. The stone of the central motif weighs 69 carats. The group of sapphires is of a deep and dense color that is particularly rare.

FACING PAGE
Parure of pear-shape D color I flawless diamonds.

are carriers of this magnificence and their perfection is the culmination of a life of exacting research. Life is present in the jewels. It sparkles warmly with each movement, its beauty gushes forth provocatively with the first look, and it coils about voluptuously to better flourish. Each object has been composed around stones selected for their quality and their relation to one another. On their own, the gems are already exceptional. The art of Alexandre Reza consists in gathering them together to set them off of one another, as if they had been destined for each other since the beginning of time.

No detail escapes him. Each stone is placed, replaced, put in the foreground, relegated to the background, supported by another or isolated, because no stone is equal to another. If after weeks or months no better solution is found, fabrication can begin.

Today Alexandre Reza still has some jewels he is not sufficiently satisfied with to execute. One day, inspiration and a brainstorm will find the definitive place for each of those stones even if he has to refashion the original model. Once the risks and the technical difficulties of production have been resolved, the jewel will come to life and will take on its intended motion, achieve a harmonious balance and remain eternally sublime.

Boucheron

Firmly established in the traditions of exquisite French jewelry, Boucheron's legacy still flourishes today as the mark of refined elegance and style. Founded during France's Second Empire, in the midst of a period of elaborate and ornate design, Frédéric Boucheron was the first to move jewelry forward into a more modern style: with designs based in nature, his sinuous, graceful creations immediately brought the attention of both the aristocracy and the new haute bourgeoisie. This was Paris' heyday. With the coronation of Napoleon III in 1852, the great city entered an era of remarkable wealth and vibrancy. Diamonds, gold and jewels flowed through Paris just as quickly as the currents of the Seine — there was a tremendous passion for jewels, and conditions were ripe for one of the greatest contributors in the world of jewelry to emerge.

ABOVE
Diamond and sapphire clip earrings on yellow gold. The sapphire pendants total 13 carats.

FACING PAGE
Diamond and sapphire necklace on yellow gold. The sapphire pendant weighs 15 carats.

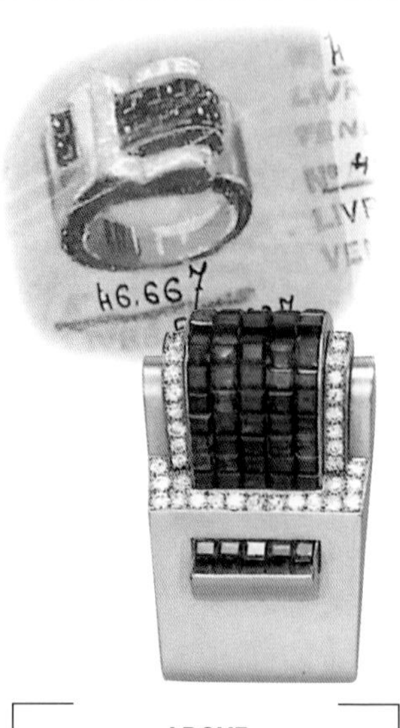

ABOVE
Sketches from inventory books of the two pieces shown below. A bangle decorated with invisibly set sapphire motifs framed by brilliant diamonds. Mounted in gold and platinum. 1939. A clip in the same style, 1939.

UPPER LEFT
Place Vendôme.

INSET
Frédéric Boucheron. Portrait by Aimé Morot, 1895.

LOWER LEFT
Illustration by Fonseca. Elegant women admiring a Boucheron window display, 1900.

BOTTOM
Snood of gold net decorated with diamonds.

The legacy of Boucheron began to take shape when the house's founder, Frédéric Boucheron, was a mere fourteen years old. An apprentice to renowned jeweler Jules Chaise, Boucheron honed his own emerging talents while running errands to earn his wages. By the age of twenty, Boucheron had graduated to salesman at the prestigious house of Tixier-Deschamps in the Palais-Royal quarter of Paris. When Deschamps took his retirement, Boucheron told the famous jeweler of his desire to establish his own shop. Deschamps brushed off his young subordinate's yearnings, saying, "Mr. Frédéric is an excellent shop assistant, but he is not cut out to be the proprietor of a business." Fortunately, Frédéric paid no attention to his former employer. Instead, at the age of twenty-eight, he set out to turn the jewelry world upside down with his own designs.

Shying away from the audacious opulence so characteristic of the latter half of the nineteenth century, Frédéric ignored the blinding displays of garish stones, stunning only for their sheer size and extravagance. Instead, Boucheron produced perfection. Selecting exclusively from the highest caliber stones — a practice the house has maintained to the present day — he applied a delicate touch, creating masterpieces of simple elegance. Boucheron brought to life the suppleness and symmetrical grace of nature in his jeweled flowers, animals and fruits. He pored over the flood of diamonds available from the newly excavated South African mines, at the same time accenting his pieces with more organic elements such as ivory and wood. Possessed of an insatiably curious and creative temperament, Boucheron was always among the first to incorporate new materials. In fact, he pioneered the art of plique-à-jour, an enameling technique that gives an open-backed piece the appearance of stained glass. With his consummate and exacting eye for detail, Boucheron also made significant advances in the public presentation of fine jewels. Not content to let his beautiful creations rest flat against glass shelves, he became the first

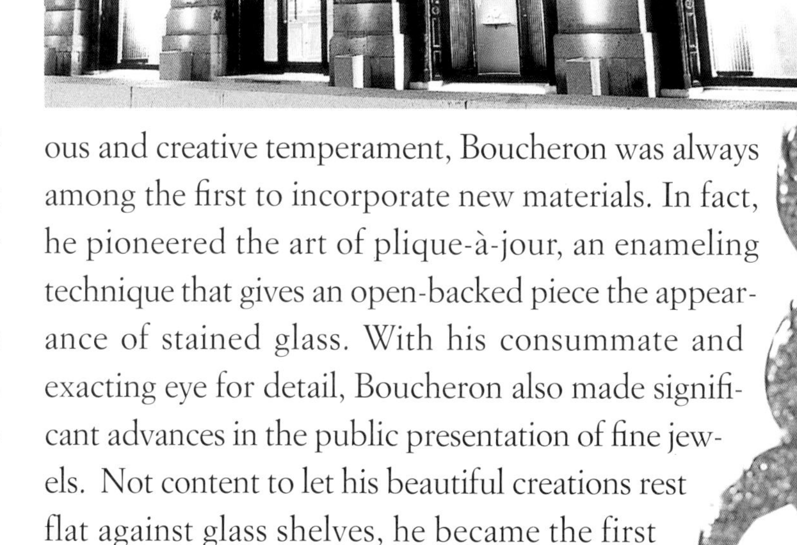

ABOVE
Illustration by Gaynon. Boucheron's "feathers," from *L'Album du Figaro*, 1951.

ABOVE RIGHT
Boucheron in Paris.

RIGHT
"Lierre" necklace and ring of rubies and diamonds set in gold.

to produce lush displays of jewels, propped up on velvet. The wonderment of Boucheron's new presentation style drew hordes of window-shoppers, clients and, ultimately, other jewelers who were compelled to follow the young upstart's lead or risk bankruptcy.

ABOVE
Diamond clip earrings on platinum and gray gold.

ABOVE LEFT
Diamond and gold bracelets.

BELOW LEFT
"Line" bracelets set with baguette-cut stones: 33 carats of sapphires, 32 carats of emeralds and 28 carats of rubies.

By the dawn of the 1870s, the clamor for Boucheron had only increased and the doors were opened to an elegant display shop on Rue de Valois. The new shop was colossal in size, filling four arcades; in comparison, L'Escalier de Cristal, the grand-dame of houses at the Palais Royal, had only three. To maintain Boucheron's trademark high standards of presentation, the revered decorator Henri Penon was asked to oversee the creation of the new space. His installation, which included cascades of chandeliers, bronze furniture and rich undertones of mahogany, made the new home of Boucheron an instant and overwhelming success.

Everything touched by Boucheron caused a sensation. In 1867, with the premiere of his jewels at the Universal Exposition, he won a gold medal for pieces in the revivalist Marie Antoinette and Campana styles. Tiffany's in New York extolled the jeweler's talents to American heiresses and succeeded in selling an ornate sapphire-and-diamond necklace to Mrs. Clarence Mackay, no stranger to the jewelry trade herself: her grandfather-in-law having discovered the world's richest silver vein in the Nevada desert. The largest of the necklace's seemingly countless sapphires weighed 159 carats, and the stunning ensemble elevated the name of Boucheron to legendary status in the American market.

Boucheron also took center stage during the very public rivalry between two heavily jeweled members of Parisian high society. La Belle Otéro — mistress of King Leopold of Belgium — and her competitor Liane de Pougy were both sworn devotees of Bouch-

ABOVE
Necklace made of gray cultured pearls. Clip earrings made of cultured pearls and diamonds.

RIGHT ABOVE
Ring with diamonds set in yellow gold.

RIGHT BELOW
Ring set with rubellite and emerald in yellow gold.

LEFT
Three rings: rubies set in gold; diamond baguettes set in platinum; yellow diamonds set in gold.

eron's creations. One evening, La Belle Otéro hushed the room at the fashionable Maxim's when she arrived in a dazzling display of diamonds. Adorned with a regal array of brooches, necklaces and rings, she waited for de Pougy with smug satisfaction. Late into the evening's festivities, de Pougy breezed into the room in a simple black dress. She wore no jewelry, but was followed by her servant, who was suspiciously cloaked. As de Pougy took a triumphant seat, the servant's cape was removed to reveal every item of jewelry from de Pougy's exorbitant and very extensive collection. All Maxim's erupted in applause and Otéro stormed from the room.

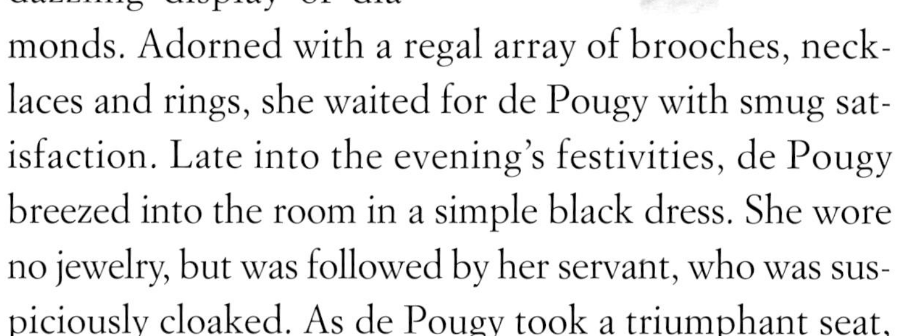

With his knack for anticipating and harnessing the fashion of the moment while at the same time dictating trends, Boucheron cultivated an impressive following; among the luminous devotees of the house of Boucheron were the Vanderbilts, Queen Isabella II of Spain, Grand Duchess Maria Alexandrovna and

ABOVE LEFT
"Axelle" rings. Diamonds on gray gold. Blue, yellow and pink sapphires on gray gold. Sapphire center and diamonds on gray gold.

ABOVE RIGHT
"Anais" rings with sapphire centers.

CENTER
Turtle brooches in diamond setting with yellow and white gold.

LEFT
Diamond and yellow gold bracelet.

Alexandra Feodorovna, wife of Tsar Nicholas II. All sought Boucheron's famed creativity and stylistic flair that kept his work on the cutting edge.

In 1893, Boucheron moved to Paris' Place Vendôme, now the world's epicenter of haute joaillerie. It was one of many precedent setting moves: Boucheron became the first jewelry house to occupy this hallowed corner of Paris. From that moment, the jeweler imprinted itself on every generation; from the New Look in the 1940s to its jewelry of today which continues to cause a stir. One of Boucheron's blue diamond rings set a world blue diamond per-carat record when it was auctioned for $2.48 million. It is testimony to his lasting influence that Frédéric Boucheron's legacy of refined elegance, the use of only the finest materials and an almost clairvoyant approach to the future of style have survived to the dawn of the twenty-first century. In the introduction to *Boucheron*, the 1988 history of the legendary house, Alain Boucheron described what may be the company's secret for success, and the essential reason that the house of Boucheron has captivated the sensibilities of the world's most glamorous women for nearly 150 years: "A jeweler can present a woman with a complement to that quality which makes her unique among women — an echo of her own beauty."

ABOVE
"Half bead" bracelets in yellow gold and diamonds, and in white gold.

RIGHT
"Caroline" rings. Emerald surrounded by sapphires. Ruby surrounded by yellow sapphire. Yellow sapphire surrounded by rubies.

LEFT
Collection of rings set in platinum.

Carrera y Carrera

BY BRILLIANTLY TRANSFORMING THE PRECEPTS OF JEWELRY STYLES, the House of Carrera y Carrera reaches beyond the traditional craft and assumes a leading role in the world of fine arts. Their tiny works are simultaneously sculpture — and jewelry. The images reduced in size, yet not diminished in impact. Worked in the finest gold and gems, gorgeously vivid and precise. Pieces of sculpture that dangle gently on a slender neck or ride boldly on a graceful finger, they are images that touch, stop and start the heart and mind at once. Since its inception in 1885, Carrera y Carrera's story has been an epic of creative evolution and worldwide expansion. Carrera y Carrera, today Spain's leading jeweler, has nurtured the success of its art within the family. It began with Jose Esteban, an accomplished gem cutter who learned his art from Parisian masters. Esteban expanded the business to include his two nephews, Saturio and Pedro Carrera.

LEFT
"Cupido Pensante" a limited edition timepiece sculptured in18K gold-plated silver and mounted on a lapis lazuli-blue base with quatz movement.

FACING PAGE
A necklace of panthers and diamonds in determnined elegance. A total 12.38 carats of daimonds.

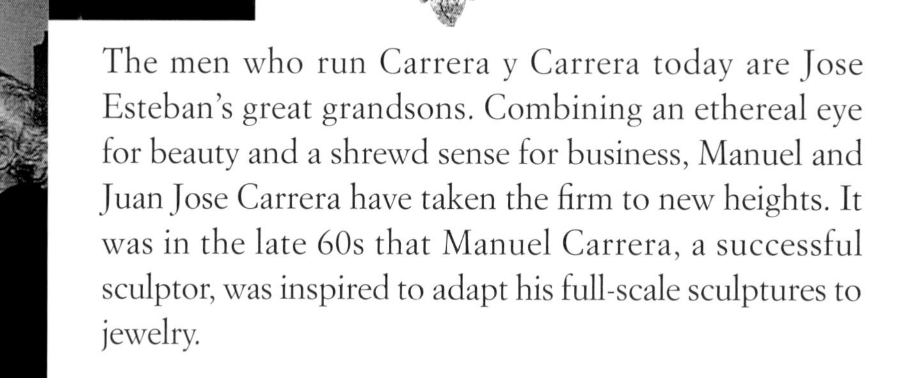

ABOVE
Queen Sofia of Spain at the official presentation of the Carrera y Carrera Arch in commemoration of the Discovery of the Americas. The presentation was held at The Royal Palace in Madrid.

ABOVE CENTER
Mr. Manuel Carrera with visiting Japanese dignitaries.

ABOVE RIGHT
Eagle necklace in 18K gold with cultured pearls, diamonds, emeralds and sapphire eyes

RIGHT
Mr. Manuel Carrera offers the Carrera y Carrera award to Placido Domingo. The sculpture depicts Placido Domingo in the role of Othello. (1995) 925mm. Silver and quartz.

BELOW RIGHT
"Caballos," a limited-edition quartz-movement timepiece. 18K gold-plated silver on a Jasper-red base.

The men who run Carrera y Carrera today are Jose Esteban's great grandsons. Combining an ethereal eye for beauty and a shrewd sense for business, Manuel and Juan Jose Carrera have taken the firm to new heights. It was in the late 60s that Manuel Carrera, a successful sculptor, was inspired to adapt his full-scale sculptures to jewelry.

Together, the three rode the currents of fate into worldwide prominence — executing prestigious commissions from the Spanish government, including Queen Fabiola's exquisitely crafted crown and the flawless, gem-coated Sword of Victory, in which the Spanish provinces are worked in a spectacular feat of artistry.

"When Carrera y Carrera started, the jewelry of the period was very similar. We decided to create our own revolutionary style," he recalls. His cousin, Juan Jose Carrera, an astute and successful businessman, was excited by the concept and the two men organized a team of expert designers. They joined forces with Carlos Mellado as design and modeling director and Antonio Calvo as production director.

RIGHT, CLOCKWISE FROM ABOVE LEFT
Saturio Esteban, Manuel Carrera's Great Grandfather; Jose Esteban, Great Uncle of Manuel Carrera and Juan Jose; José Carrera and Saturio Esteban, uncles (from the father's side).

LEFT
Eagle necklace in 18K gold with south sea pearls, diamonds and ruby eyes

BELOW
One-of-a-kind Pegasus necklace, with a beautiful square cut emerald weighing 72.5 carats.

Instead of starting small, Carrera y Carrera chose to prove their artistry from the outset by developing an entire collection based on the subject most difficult to sculpt — the human hands. The hands in all their variations — clasping pearls, cradling diamonds, grasping a watch face — were executed with breathtaking virtuosity. Perfectly detailed palms, shiny nails and all the wit, originality and astonishing grace that the human hand communicates. The hands became known as the "Caress" Collection — for years Carrera y Carrera's trademark — which remains one of the company's most popular creations.

The Carrera y Carrera team crafted a new corporate image, establishing themselves as a world-renowned jeweler by continuing with this revolution of style. They did not depart from the tried-and-true methodologies. Instead, they incorporated age-old techniques. The two most prominent hallmarks of Carrera y Carrera jewelry are their matte finish — a closely guarded family secret — which suggests a wash of warm, late-day sunlight, and the intricate detailing of the work, which creates the grace of a tiny sculpture.

But from where does the inspiration for these unusual themes come? "Carrera y Carrera," explains Manuel

LEFT ABOVE, CENTER AND BELOW
From the "Noe" collection: Dolphin bracelet, ring and necklace in gold.

RIGHT
Goddess bracelet with amethyst in gold from the "Masquerade" set.

BELOW RIGHT
Sueno braceleet with ruby and diamonds from the "Masquerade" set.

Carrera, "is inspired by themes that are able to awaken a very deep admiration for the animal kingdom, feelings of love and passion, and of mythological and romantic themes in history." Amid the dazzling success of the "Caress" line, designers expanded the collection to include mythological characters — among them Prometheus, Bacchus and Pegasus — various animals renowned for their strength and grace, and the human form.

Among the jewelry lines you will find the "Pantera" collection, a panther's head, chosen as a symbol of strength and agility, while the "Caballos" collection portrays galloping horses in a strikingly original, richly energetic and a stunning display of magic and portent.

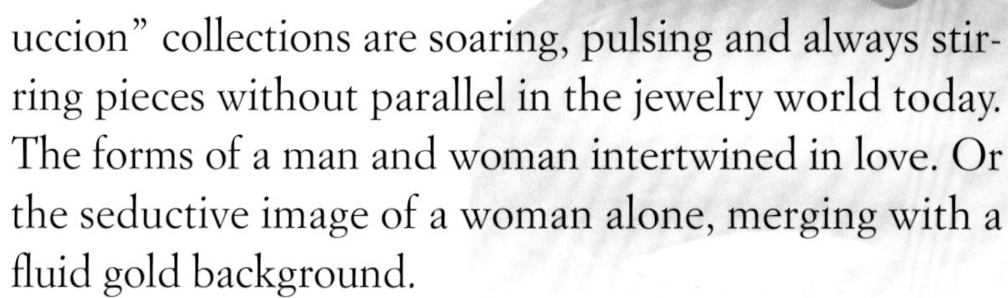

The "Eros" and "Seduccion" collections are soaring, pulsing and always stirring pieces without parallel in the jewelry world today. The forms of a man and woman intertwined in love. Or the seductive image of a woman alone, merging with a fluid gold background.

The artistry of this jewelry has for years attracted serious collectors from many continents. They are drawn not only by the gold and gems, not only by the consummate craftsmanship, but by the notion that these are one-of-a-kind works of art. Although Carrera y Carrera has more than 12,000 designs, each is engraved with a unique serial number in order to ensure authenticity.

The creative process for each piece, according to Manuel Carrera, is exhaustive. For each piece, no matter how simple, the work does not begin until several sketches are executed and approved. The actual assemblage can take from a day to weeks. For example, a piece commemorating Cricket designed for De Beers' president, Nicholas Oppenheimer, is five feet, three inches tall and nearly as wide. It weighs 600 pounds and took 6,000 hours to create. In celebration of the

discovery of the Americas, Carrera y Carrera presented Queen Sofia of Spain with the "Arc," an intricately sculpted series of panels that took an amazing 12,000 hours to produce.

Manuel Carrera finds inspiration for his work everywhere. He has that uncommon ability to see beyond the quiet beauty of the commonplace, to explore worlds of infinite variation. He can be transfixed by the possibilities of the most unassuming objects, said Roberto Cristobal, president of Carrera y Carrera, Inc. Once, during a visit to Hawaii, Mr. Carrera was unusually quiet during a business dinner. When a shop owner inquired as to what was occupying his thoughts, Mr. Carrera said he was considering creating a Santa Claus sculpture with the oyster shells that remained on the plates from the appetizer course. Laughing, the shop owner challenged him to do just that. Proving again, of course, his particular ability to marry pathos and humor, Mr. Carrera carried through his whimsical vision and the Santa Claus is proudly displayed — and sold — in the Hawaiian shop today.

ABOVE
Horse necklaces from the "Noe" collection. Gold set with citrine, pavé diamonds or amethyst.

LEFT
Rings from the Sentimientos Collection. Each ring bears diamonds from .25 to 2 carats.

BELOW
Bracelet from the "Panther" collection in gold with diamonds.

It is the force of style, matched only by its breath of experience and depth of creative thought, that has led many museums around the world to collect and display Carrera y Carrera works. They can be found at the Royal Palace in Madrid, the White House in Washington, D.C., The Yamagoshi Prefectural Museum in Japan and the Hadley Museum in Kentucky.

The company also takes pride in recognizing citizens for their individual contributions to humanity by awarding sculptures. Recipients include: Placido Domingo, whom they presented with a sculpture of himself as Othello; former United States President Ronald Reagan, who is depicted as a cowboy riding a bucking bronco; Mieczyslav Rostropovich, the former director of the Philharmonic

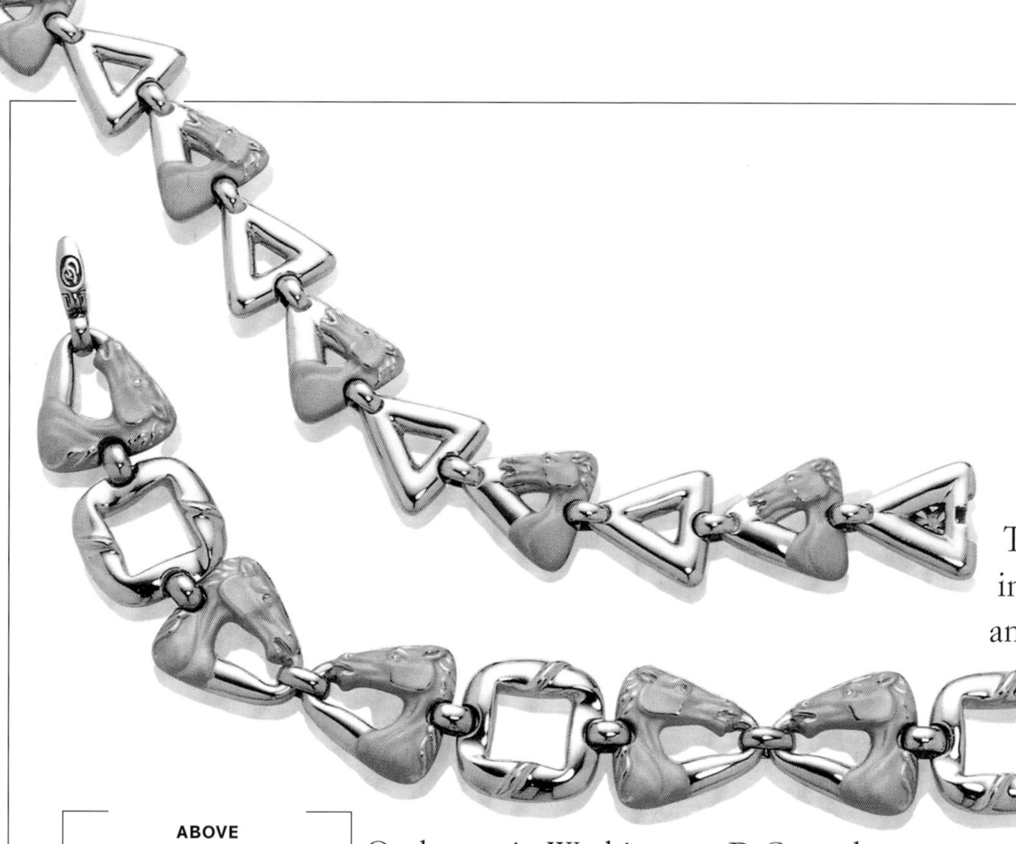

ABOVE
Horse bracelets in two sizes from the "Compass" horses collection.
BELOW RIGHT
Limited edition watches, automatic Swiss movement and 18K gold and diamonds. Alligator strap.
FACING PAGE
Soldier, 18K gold and diamond with ruby accents. Center fresh water pearl. A one-of-a-kind from the Private Collection.

Orchestra in Washington, D.C., and former Argentinean President Raul Alfonsin.

More recently, Carrera y Carrera has undertaken one of its most impressive projects — designing the main door of Madrid's Cathedral, "la Puerta de Santa Maria." It will take a full ton of silver to create the eight-feet tall engravings that will depict the history of Madrid. Another mammoth project stands in Carrera y Carrera's Madrid factory — a life-size reproduction of a sculpture dating to Celtic period of approximately 400 B.C., found in Spain by archeologists. Carrera y Carrera completely recreated the artifact, according to specifics provided by the archeologists.

The future of this venerable jewelry firm is now in the hands of a new generation. Like the gold and precious stones of his work, Manuel Carrera says the future is gleaming. The company continues to expand, moving recently for the second time to larger quarters in Madrid.

But the two men who began running Spain's most successful jewelry company a generation ago will never forget their roots and the quiet influence of the great masters. And to remind them of the past, they hang on still to the quaint shop in the historic center of Madrid on Santa Maria Road where three generations, and soon four, will have pursued their art.

"Our desire is for the pieces we create to be considered not as a symbol, not as an article of luxury, but as an authentic art piece," said Manuel Carrera, a philosophy he says is embraced by the next generation. And as such, it will be an art that never loses its fire.

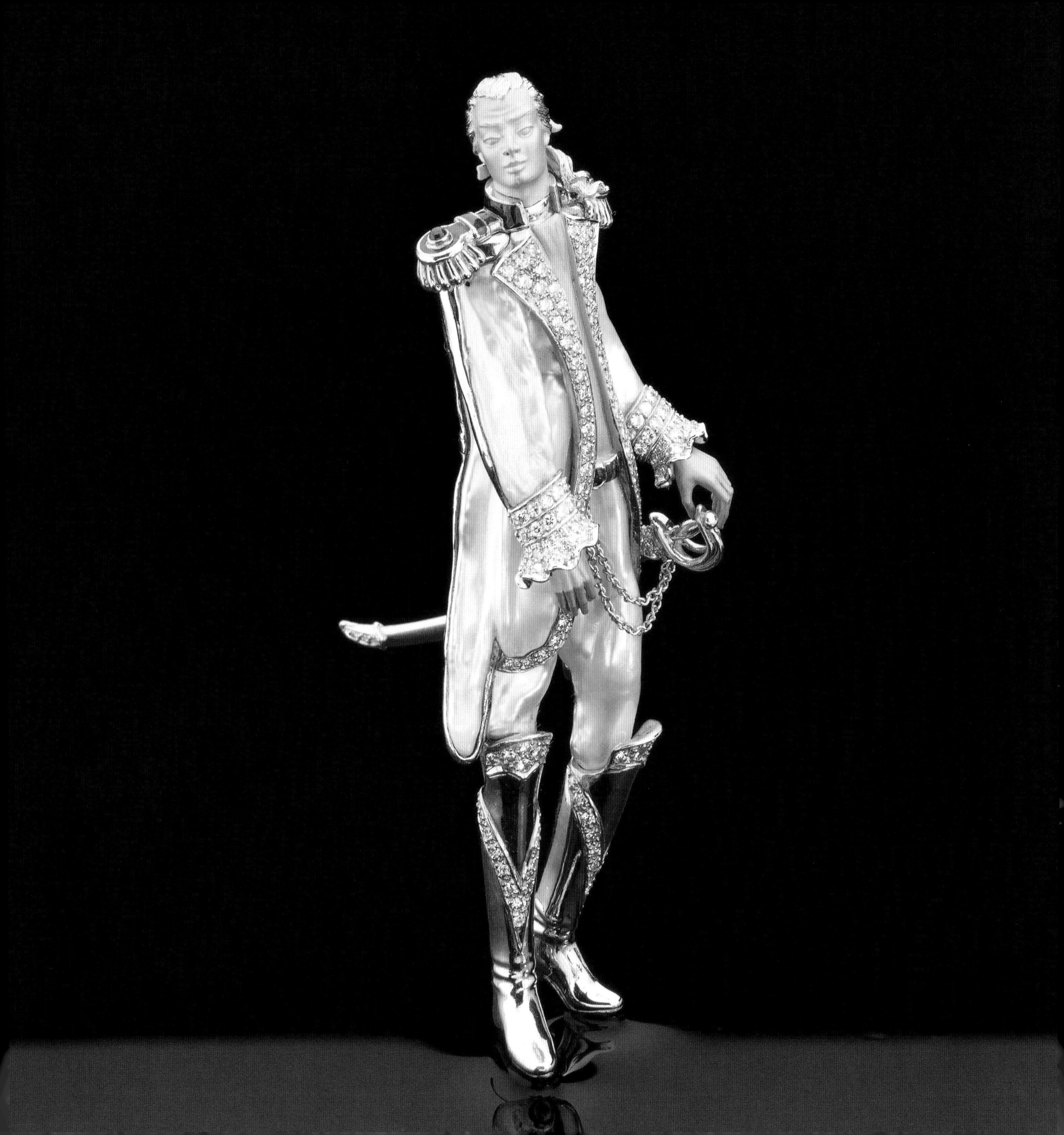

Chanel Fine Jewelry

Multicolored church windows and mosaics of the Byzantine era, Russian icons, vibrant colors of semiprecious stones — all served as inspiration to Coco Chanel and all are revealed through the CHANEL Fine Jewelry Collection today. Exquisite, one-of-a-kind stones reign supreme in entrancing designs; in one case, an immense 11-carat pink sapphire is surrounded by pear-shaped diamonds in a trembleuse setting that shimmers with every gesture. In other jewels, Mademoiselle's signature emerges unmistakably, as with the Jacquard ring, in which princess-cut diamonds encircle an unusually exquisite cabochon sapphire. In an impressive show of virtuosity, peridots, rhodolites and amethysts dance amidst a tangle of gold, bound by gold crosses pavéd in diamonds in an extraordinary piece named the Venetian necklace. Accompanied by matching earrings and bracelet, the parure gracefully captures the spirit of one of Coco Chanel's favorite cities.

LEFT
18K white gold "Starry Night" earclips with diamonds and channel-set buff-top sapphires.

FACING PAGE
"Starry Night" necklace in 18K white gold, channel-set buff-top sapphires and diamonds.

CHANEL fine jewelry has long reflected Coco's heritage, which stretches across Europe from Italy to Russia, and the influence of her celebrated lovers with whom she explored the art of refined living. Her innovations in jewelry and fashion expressed her particular genius; her ability to draw from different cultures and different sources, from the very humble to the exceptionally luxurious, led her to create a personal style that would define elegance and sophistication for decades to come.

More than sixty years ago, at the peak of her career as a fashion designer, Chanel presented a jewelry exhibit that single-handedly modernized diamond jewelry. At this event, staged in her home in November of 1932, Chanel unveiled a breakthrough collection. In one presentation, a diamond necklace was splayed across a lady's shoulders; in another, dozens of small diamonds dangled over a woman's forehead in what was called "Chanel fringe." This last item was so unusual that it drew enormous crowds of the jewelers and journalists in attendance. Startling for its innovation, the collection also stirred interest among those who knew Chanel and had heard her say, more than once, that "a woman should only wear colored stones," (when she is not wearing pearls, that is). However, as she noted in explaining her new approach, the diamond is the most concentrated form of luxury. Certainly, diamonds contrasted perfectly with her preferred black wardrobe.

Though the exhibition marked the official beginning of Chanel's jewelry collection, she had been creating jewelry for herself for years, often inventing new pieces and redesigning jewelry given to her by her distinguished lovers, the

LEFT
18K white gold, Colombian emerald and diamond "Trembleuse" ring.

FAR LEFT
Coco Chanel aboard a gondola in one of her favorite cities, Venice. Below, the Piazza San Marco in Venice.

CENTER LEFT
18K white gold and diamonds "Kaleidoscope" ring.

BELOW LEFT
Interior of Mademoiselle Chanel's salon.

BELOW
18K white gold, diamond and cabochon sapphire "Galaxie" ring.

BOTTOM CENTER
Magnificent 18K yellow gold, pink sapphire and diamond "Trembleuse" ring.

Grand Duke Dmitri of Russia and the Duke of Westminster. Chanel had long since established a greater role for pearls in fine jewelry; the by-the-yard pearls that she wore religiously became a model of elegance for many Parisian women. Rare is the photo of Mademoiselle in which she is seen without gems strung voluminously around her neck and at her wrists. Particularly beautiful are her signature cuffs bearing the Maltese Cross, created for her by Fulco de Verdura, an Italian count of phenomenal creative talent. When Chanel set up a shop in Paris to develop new items, Verdura oversaw design, helping her to launch the next vogue in jewelry: long chains and a mix of colorful gems.

ABOVE
"Venetian" collar in 18K yellow gold, faceted colored stones and diamonds.

LEFT
"Venetian" earclips in 18K yellow gold, colored stones and diamonds.

RIGHT
"Venetian" cuff bracelet in 18K yellow gold, colored stones and diamonds.

Chanel's frequent use of precious and semi-precious gems was inspired by her many visits to Venice with the Grand Duke Dmitri. The two gravitated toward the radiant Byzantine jewels in the Treasury of St. Mark's. So intense was her attraction to these classic pieces, Chanel fashioned numerous crosses, rings, and earrings in a bold, Byzantine-influenced style.

ABOVE
18K white gold and diamond "Fringe" necklace.

LEFT
18K white gold, diamond and cultured pearl "Volute" earclips.

BELOW
18K white gold, black onyx and diamond "Harmonie" bracelet

BOTTOM RIGHT
18K white gold and diamond "Globe" rings in black Tahitian and white South Sea pearl.

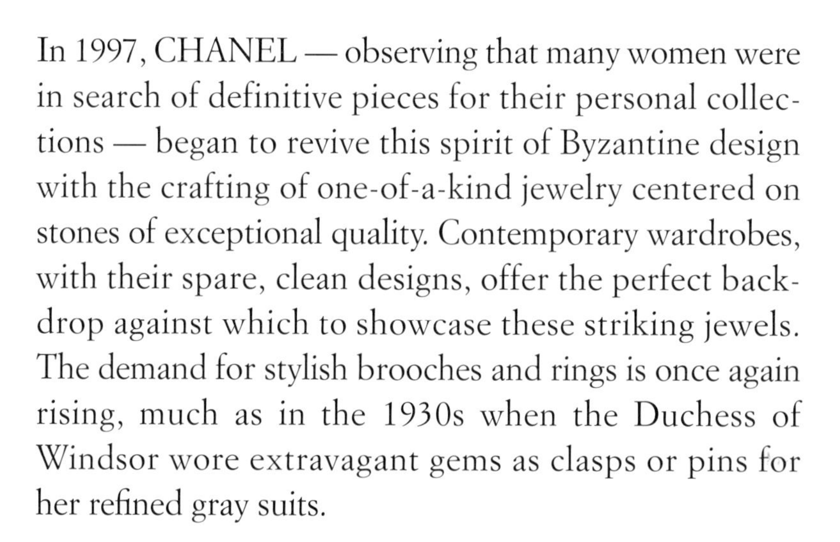

In 1997, CHANEL — observing that many women were in search of definitive pieces for their personal collections — began to revive this spirit of Byzantine design with the crafting of one-of-a-kind jewelry centered on stones of exceptional quality. Contemporary wardrobes, with their spare, clean designs, offer the perfect backdrop against which to showcase these striking jewels. The demand for stylish brooches and rings is once again rising, much as in the 1930s when the Duchess of Windsor wore extravagant gems as clasps or pins for her refined gray suits.

The rings in the CHANEL contemporary collection display gems of extraordinary size and quality. A deep blue tanzanite stone with overtones of purple is accompanied by a kaleidoscope pattern of diamonds in a one-of-a-kind ring that was created for the opening of the CHANEL Place Vendôme boutique. In the Jacquard series, which features patterns of princess-cut diamonds that echo Chanel's signature quilting, each ring is individually created, using the most sumptuous cabochon

gems. The diamonds, too, are of top-quality and the result is artful jewelry of extraordinary distinction.

CHANEL chooses its Tahitian South Sea pearls in gray and white with the same degree of care. In a cool, flowing rope that defines the luxuriousness of pearls, the treasures from the sea are perfectly matched in color and size, ranging from 11 to 15.5 millimeters. The captivating beauty of these pearl ropes makes it immediately clear why Coco Chanel was so passionate about pearls — and why she didn't hesitate to use cultured pearls when they first appeared in the 1930s. The collection also features globe rings, with large pearls seemingly raised upwards by shooting diamond stars. These stunning rings work in perfect rapport with the elegant string of pearls.

ABOVE
Interwined ropes of Tahitian and South Sea cultured pearls with 18K white gold and diamond "Camellia" clasps.

TOP RIGHT
Gabrielle "Coco" Chanel.

BOTTOM RIGHT
18K yellow gold, ruby, sapphire and emerald "Rooster" brooch with feather plumage and freshwater pearl drops.

Animals of both land and sea were long considered powerful talismans by Chanel. Born under the zodiac sign of Leo, she prized the lion and

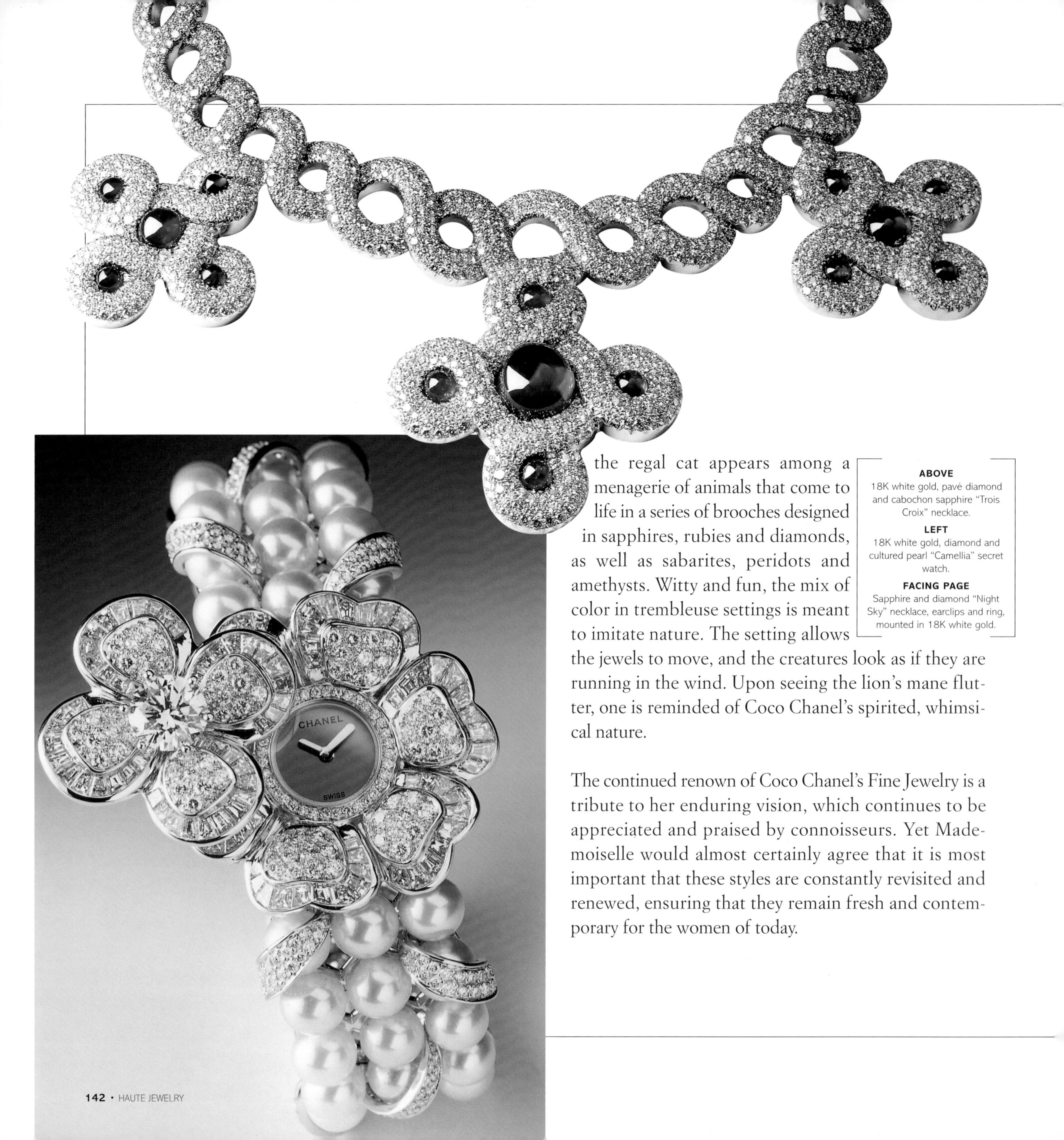

the regal cat appears among a menagerie of animals that come to life in a series of brooches designed in sapphires, rubies and diamonds, as well as sabarites, peridots and amethysts. Witty and fun, the mix of color in trembleuse settings is meant to imitate nature. The setting allows the jewels to move, and the creatures look as if they are running in the wind. Upon seeing the lion's mane flutter, one is reminded of Coco Chanel's spirited, whimsical nature.

ABOVE
18K white gold, pavé diamond and cabochon sapphire "Trois Croix" necklace.

LEFT
18K white gold, diamond and cultured pearl "Camellia" secret watch.

FACING PAGE
Sapphire and diamond "Night Sky" necklace, earclips and ring, mounted in 18K white gold.

The continued renown of Coco Chanel's Fine Jewelry is a tribute to her enduring vision, which continues to be appreciated and praised by connoisseurs. Yet Mademoiselle would almost certainly agree that it is most important that these styles are constantly revisited and renewed, ensuring that they remain fresh and contemporary for the women of today.

Chaumet

The history of the prestigious House of Chaumet spans two centuries, during which time the fame of its jewelry has spread from France to the rest of Europe and finally to the rest of the world. Today, Chaumet produces the finest of Haute Joaillerie, exquisite works of art prized by those of uncompromising taste.

LEFT
Ethnie clip earrings in white gold with pavé diamonds and two oval diamond pendants.

FACING PAGE
Cadenas necklace in yellow gold with pavé diamonds crowned with a 14.6 carat emerald.

ABOVE
Long *Bayadère* in seed pearls, diamonds and sapphires, 1914. Chaumet Museum, Paris.

RIGHT
Replica of the wedding parure of Marie-Louise of Habsburg-Lorraine, Archduchess of Austria. When Napoleon commissioned Nitot to create this parure, the jeweler was highly flattered. He made two similar parures, one in rubies and diamonds was delivered to the Emperor (it was later destroyed), the other parure in garnets and white sapphires was kept by Nitot. 1810. Chaumet Museum, Paris.

ABOVE RIGHT
Design for an emerald and diamonds bodice ornament, 1910. Chaumet Museum, Paris. The design was used as the cover of the Chaumet book published in 1995.

LEFT
An advertisement from the 1920s. Chaumet Museum, Paris.

The Chaumet tradition begins in 1783 with Marie-Etienne Nitot, accepted that year as a master goldsmith. Before long, he had established an aristocratic clientele with court connections. The earliest surviving example of his work is an exquisitely crafted memorial box from 1789 for the Marquise de Lawoestine, who had died during childbirth.

During the French Revolution, the luxury trades were hard hit. Many workshops were forced to close due to labor shortages and lack of orders. Some artisans managed to stay in business by making ceremonial weapons, and military accessories that required the skill of fine craftsmen. Nitot and his son,

FAR LEFT
Inès Sastre wears a long necklace from the *Fidelité* collection. Precious and sensual, this long necklace in white gold is set with over 15 carats of white diamonds, with a fall created by two pavé diamond buttons.

LEFT
Two *Fidelité* rings in white gold set with diamonds, the most precious one is crowned with a 3.86 carat oval diamond.

Francois-Regnault, survived the Revolution, and were chosen to mount the Regent, the most important diamond in the State treasury, onto Napoleon's Consular Sword. Nitot & Fils, as the firm was now called, went on to create important examples of insignia jewelry in the Empire style, as well as some of the earliest pieces in the Romantic style that followed.

When Marie-Etienne Nitot died in 1809, his son was well prepared to take over the business. Francois-Regnault Nitot had both the talent and the business sense to take advantage of his position, and became a frequent supplier to the Emperor by appointment. It was a time when the court of Napoleon was demanding work of an elegance and luxury that would impress all of Europe. Nitot Père & Fils made their fortune by satisfying the Emperor's wishes.

None of Francois-Regnault Nitot's children continued in the jewelry trade, so when he retired, he passed along the business to his foreman, Jean-Baptiste Fossin. Fossin, a draughtsman and painter as well as a jeweler, encouraged his employees to turn to the nearby Bibliotheque

FAR RIGHT
Ophée necklace in yellow gold with pavé diamonds on an interchangeable red satin choker.
RIGHT
Homage à Venise rings in white or yellow gold with pavé diamonds. Small and large models shown.

Royal and the Louvre as sources of inspiration. In 1819, he was awarded a medal at the Exposition des Arts de l'Industrie and the firm soon regained royal patronage.

This was an era of great opportunity for France's jewelers. As new social upheavals led to a greater distribution of wealth and more widespread fortunes, the number of potential buyers for fine jewelry grew. Although the older aristocracy — still reeling from the effects of revolution and exile — moderated their luxury spending to some degree, there were others to fill the gap. There were new society figures, such as the Rothschilds, to cater to, as well as a number of wealthy foreigners. At the same time, progress in the art of refining metals was making it possible to produce jewels at lower cost. Working in the

popular styles of the period — Gothic, Renaissance, and later, Egyptian — the Fossin firm proved its ability to create a diverse array of artworks.

Fossin's son Jules was made an associate in 1832, and in 1845, took over the business. Over the next decade-and-a-half, one of Jules Fossin's most important associates was Jean-Valentin Morel, whose son Prosper took the reins of the firm in 1861. While maintaining the loyalty of the old Parisian aristocracy, Prosper Morel expanded the company's business, making frequent trips to foreign capitals to establish a new clientele.

In the last decade of the nineteenth century, the firm took on the Chaumet name under Joseph Chaumet, who married Prosper Morel's daughter. The business had passed through a slow period, but Chaumet brought new momentum, and by 1900 the company was once again flourishing and expanding. This era was one of the most creative in the firm's history. Chaumet's legendary skill at judging precious stones and pearls attracted considerable investments from bankers and other leading figures.

ABOVE RIGHT
From top to bottom, four *Goia* rings in white gold set with a pink tourmaline, an amethyst, an iolite and a citrine.

ABOVE LEFT
From *Liens de Chaumet* collection, various models in white gold with pavé diamonds.

Under Joseph Chaumet's son, Marcel, the firm continued to build on its reputation. Marcel Chaumet led the company in adapting its designs to suit the boyish

LEFT
Inès Sastre is wearing the *Fidelité* jewels. The necklace is matte yellow gold, wide and small bracelets are in polished and matte yellow gold. The interchangeable button-clasp is available in all yellow or white gold, in yellow gold with star-set diamonds or all pavé set with diamonds.

ABOVE
The *Anneau* rings collection in white gold, various sizes all gold with pavé diamonds or with star set diamonds.

fashion look of the 1920s and the more womanly silhouette of the 1930s. Cubism inspired Chaumet to create new looks in jewelry with clean, simple lines and striking geometric settings. During the art deco period, the firm explored designs based on sharp contrasts of color, involving a variety of precious and semiprecious stones. While these decades brought sometimes bewildering shifts in style, Chaumet always maintained its tradition of quality and luxury.

Today that tradition thrives under the leadership of Pierre Haquet. With each new collection from its workshops, Chaumet proves its unmatched ability to satisfy the needs and desires of the contemporary world, while remaining true to the history that has nurtured it. The latest jewels from Chaumet are a revelation in sleek, stark lines of perfect grace. One dazzling example is the Nuit d'Étè bracelet and ring in white gold sprinkled with stars, some set with diamonds.

For those who demand the ultimate in elegance, there are sophisticated updatings of traditional, timeless designs. The remarkably supple Ipanema necklace, in white gold set with diamonds and twenty-eight oval emeralds, is sure to please the most discerning eye. All of the collections evoke the vision of Marie-Etienne Nitot, whose spirit perseveres at Chaumet. Such tradition is held dear in the creation of jewels that reflect modern times.

The history that has been made at 12 Place Vendôme continues to provide a strong foundation as Chaumet enters the twenty-first century. Chaumet is a jewelrymaking legend ever in tune with the spirit of a constantly changing culture. For all those who treasure beauty and perfection, Chaumet offers jewelry to live by.

ABOVE

The *Khésis* collection of watches and jewels, available in yellow or white gold, the watches also available in steel. From left to right: *Khésis* Top Lady watch in steel with pavé diamonds, *Khésis* ring in white gold with princess-cut diamonds or all white gold.

RIGHT

Style de Chaumet rings in white or yellow gold set with an iolite, a pink tourmaline and a peridot.

Chopard

FUN, FANCIFUL JEWELRY wearable for all occasions and exquisitely crafted is the trademark of Chopard and the objective of its visionary designer, Caroline Gruosi-Scheufele. "I found jewelry to be such a serious concept, nobody dared to venture outside of this approach. I have always thought that jewelry can be fun," says Gruosi-Scheufele, who started her career at the youthful age of fifteen with the successful launch of the "Happy Diamonds" jewelry line. The inaugural item, a jolly clown with diamonds floating in its belly, has since evolved into bounteous variations throughout Chopard's collection of Haute Joaillerie and jeweled timepieces. Among the latest joyful incarnations is the "Happy Star," a limited series of 999 timepieces, each with floating diamond stars shimmering across the watche's face. The "Happy Star" was created in tribute to the Cannes Film Festival for which Chopard is an official sponsor until the millennium, a strategy pursued by Caroline Gruosi-Scheufele in her devotion to creating and marketing the world's leading exclusive jewelry.

LEFT
Earclips in 18K white and yellow gold set with white and yellow brilliants. Ring set with a heart-shaped array of 27 yellow brilliants and 198 white brilliants.

FACING PAGE
Necklace in 18K white and yellow gold set with 1,896 brilliants and 391 trapeze-cut diamonds. Hearts set with 163 yellow brilliants. Part of the "Day-Night" collection. The center of these pieces can be turned around—one side is polished, the other is set with brilliants.

As a sponsor of last year's festival, Chopard created jewels for the necks of leading celebrities and models. Caroline Gruosi-Scheufele carefully selected each item of Chopard's Haute Joaillerie for famed actresses like Gong Li, Sigourney Weaver and Isabelle Huppert and for top models Carla Bruni and Eva Herzigova.

For Chopard, a company at the center of the Haute Joaillerie world, participating in an event such as the Cannes Film Festival is a natural step. "When you see the people in the streets of Cannes, lined up in front of the red carpeted stairs, hoping to see film stars from fifty meters away... the reason they are standing there is all about dreams. I think both of our worlds are very similar in that way," explains Caroline Gruosi-Scheufele. "We create many pieces of jewelry that are very creative, that people dream of."

Caroline Gruosi-Scheufele attends to each detail with a consuming passion, and the sponsorship of the Cannes Film Festival is testimony to her devotion. Not content to sim-

LEFT TOP TO BOTTOM
French actress Isabelle Huppert, wearing a Chopard jewelry set, on the famous stairway.

Pamela Soo and her husband Jean-Hughes Anglade. She wears a Strada necklace.

Sigourney Weaver, member of the official jury of the festival, wearing a necklace from the Haute Joaillerie collection.

Chinese actress Gong Li wearing a Chopard jewelry set.

INSET
Happy Star watch, produced by Chopard specially for the Cannes Film Festival.

TOP CENTER
1998 Palme d'Or created by Chopard, official sponsor of the Cannes Film Festival.

BELOW
Caroline Gruosi-Scheufele, vice-president of Chopard.

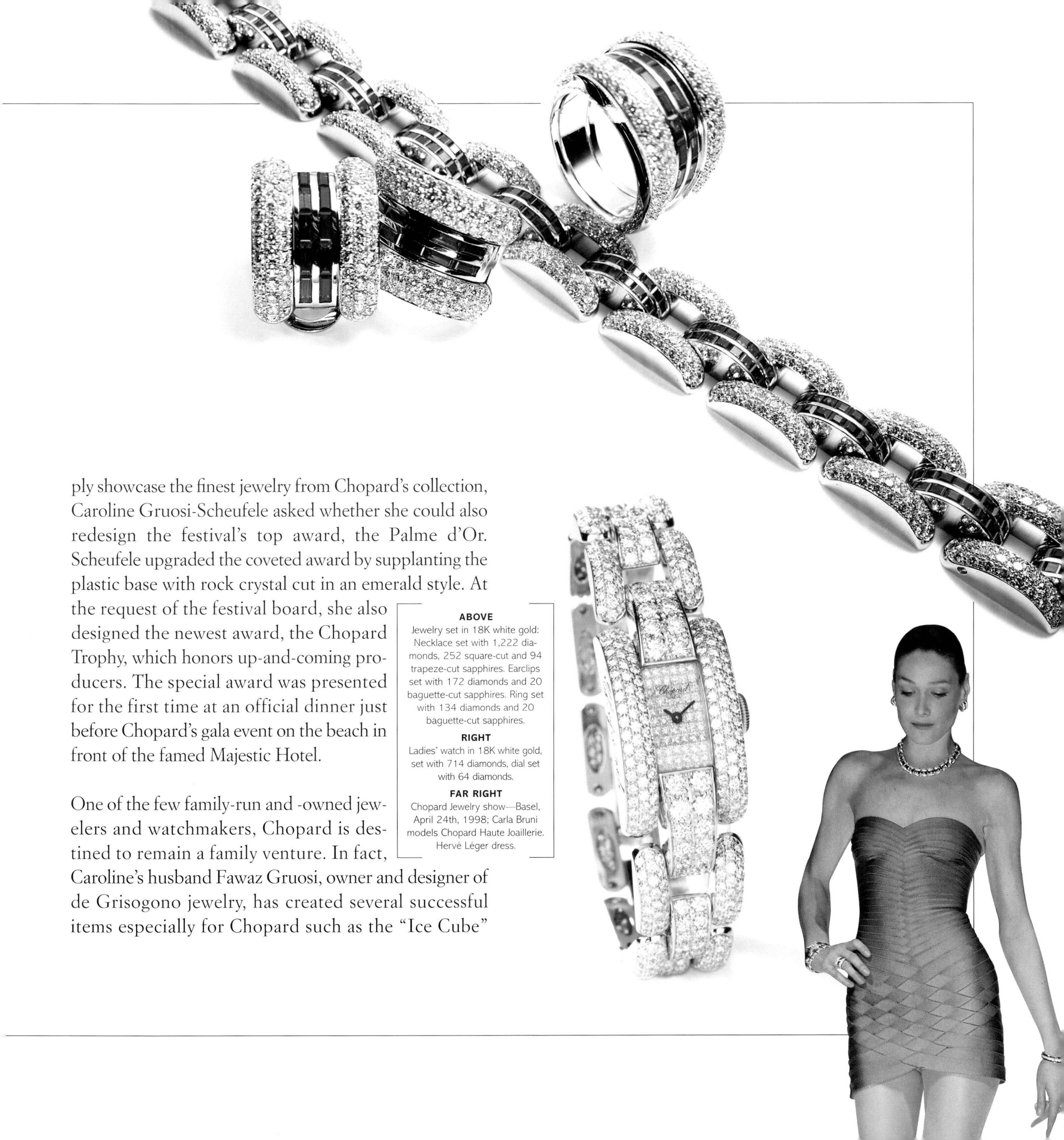

ply showcase the finest jewelry from Chopard's collection, Caroline Gruosi-Scheufele asked whether she could also redesign the festival's top award, the Palme d'Or. Scheufele upgraded the coveted award by supplanting the plastic base with rock crystal cut in an emerald style. At the request of the festival board, she also designed the newest award, the Chopard Trophy, which honors up-and-coming producers. The special award was presented for the first time at an official dinner just before Chopard's gala event on the beach in front of the famed Majestic Hotel.

ABOVE
Jewelry set in 18K white gold: Necklace set with 1,222 diamonds, 252 square-cut and 94 trapeze-cut sapphires. Earclips set with 172 diamonds and 20 baguette-cut sapphires. Ring set with 134 diamonds and 20 baguette-cut sapphires.

RIGHT
Ladies' watch in 18K white gold, set with 714 diamonds, dial set with 64 diamonds.

FAR RIGHT
Chopard Jewelry show—Basel, April 24th, 1998; Carla Bruni models Chopard Haute Joaillerie. Hervé Léger dress.

One of the few family-run and -owned jewelers and watchmakers, Chopard is destined to remain a family venture. In fact, Caroline's husband Fawaz Gruosi, owner and designer of de Grisogono jewelry, has created several successful items especially for Chopard such as the "Ice Cube"

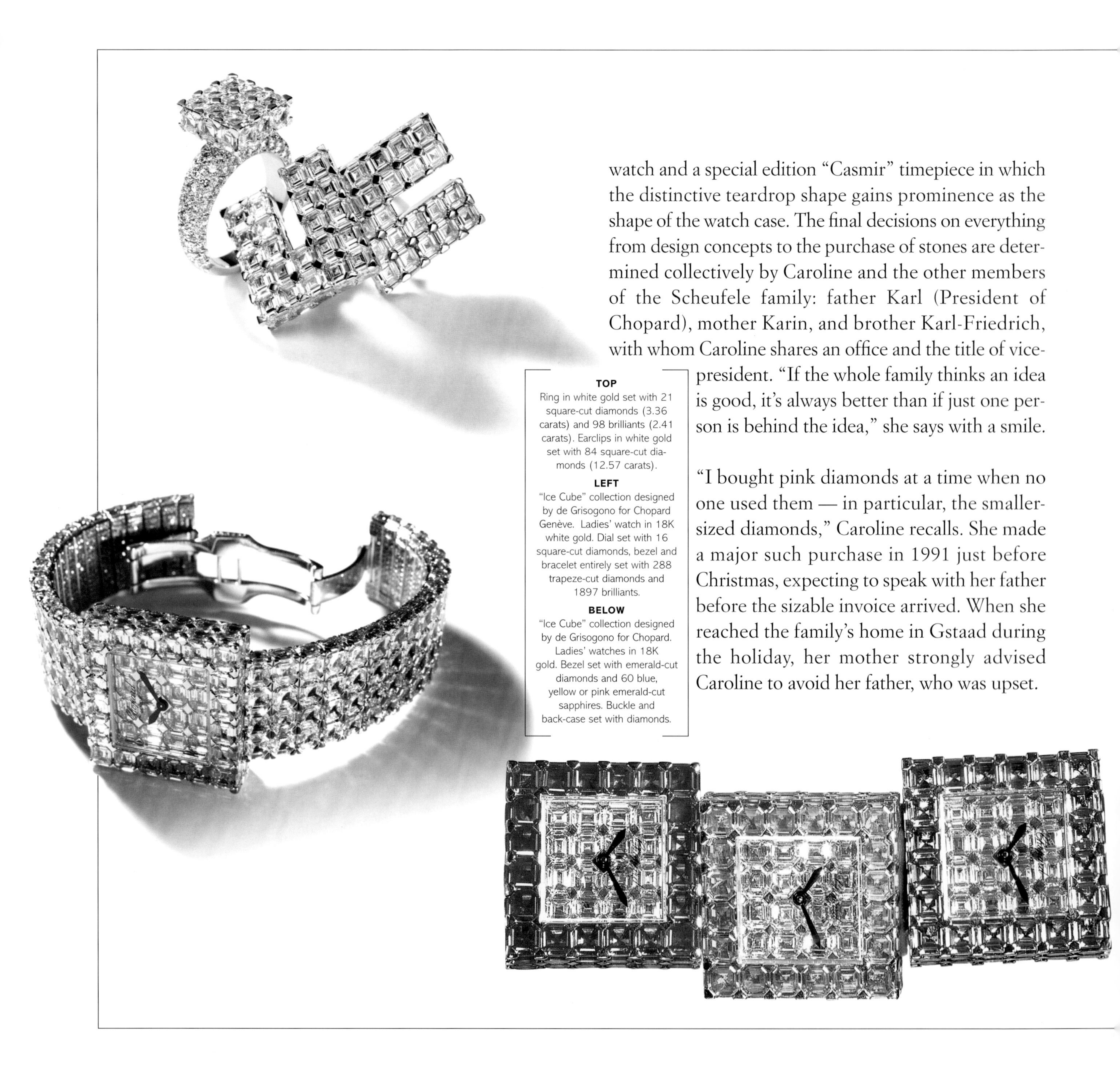

watch and a special edition "Casmir" timepiece in which the distinctive teardrop shape gains prominence as the shape of the watch case. The final decisions on everything from design concepts to the purchase of stones are determined collectively by Caroline and the other members of the Scheufele family: father Karl (President of Chopard), mother Karin, and brother Karl-Friedrich, with whom Caroline shares an office and the title of vice-president. "If the whole family thinks an idea is good, it's always better than if just one person is behind the idea," she says with a smile.

TOP
Ring in white gold set with 21 square-cut diamonds (3.36 carats) and 98 brilliants (2.41 carats). Earclips in white gold set with 84 square-cut diamonds (12.57 carats).

LEFT
"Ice Cube" collection designed by de Grisogono for Chopard Genève. Ladies' watch in 18K white gold. Dial set with 16 square-cut diamonds, bezel and bracelet entirely set with 288 trapeze-cut diamonds and 1897 brilliants.

BELOW
"Ice Cube" collection designed by de Grisogono for Chopard. Ladies' watches in 18K gold. Bezel set with emerald-cut diamonds and 60 blue, yellow or pink emerald-cut sapphires. Buckle and back-case set with diamonds.

"I bought pink diamonds at a time when no one used them — in particular, the smaller-sized diamonds," Caroline recalls. She made a major such purchase in 1991 just before Christmas, expecting to speak with her father before the sizable invoice arrived. When she reached the family's home in Gstaad during the holiday, her mother strongly advised Caroline to avoid her father, who was upset.

"At the time, the pink diamonds were five times more expensive than white diamonds, although today we pay twelve times more. I had the most terrible Christmas ever," she says. "My parents said I was crazy for spending that much. I was crying and my father told me to calm down, and he added, 'You better have a good idea.' So I said, 'I have a good idea — the diamonds are for Paris, I want to create a line called La Vie en Rose, all based on pink diamonds.' It was a desperate design, but very successful, because everyone started using pink diamonds afterward."

ABOVE
Necklace in 18K white gold with flowers set with 231 brilliants and 197 navette-cut diamonds.

RIGHT
Ring in 18K white gold with flowers set with 13 brilliants and 34 navette-cut diamonds. Earclips in 18K white gold with flowers set with 38 brilliants and 96 navette-cut diamonds.

BELOW RIGHT
Ladies' watch in 18K white gold with flowers set with 52 brilliants and 103 navette-cut diamonds. Dial set with 80 diamonds.

BELOW LEFT
Cannes Film Festival, 1998. Chopard Ambassadresses Carla Bruni and Eva Herzigova wear Chopard jewelery.

A tireless creator and prolific designer, Caroline Gruosi-Scheufele possesses a strength and certitude that belie her diminutive build. Colleagues and guests alike are welcomed with a warmth kindled by confidence and creativity. She is unrivaled among contemporary designers for her ability to single-handedly create successful lines of jewelry, from the "Happy Diamonds" collection, to the Casmir line, to the Strada collection to the La Vie en Rose line.

What is next for this inspired designer? The Pushkin collection, created in honor of Russian poet Alexander Pushkin.

Brightly colored, decorative domes towering above the Red Square provide inspiration for the Pushkin collection. Throughout the line, Scheufele has expanded the range of precious gems and stones, and the result is a vivid collection in an effusive color palette. In one piece, turquoise fills a series of inverted dome shapes, all set in white gold. The collection promises to find a happy place on Russian social agendas.

ABOVE
"Pushkin" collection earclips in 18K white gold set with 620 brilliants and two pearls.

LEFT
Casmir Collection ladies' watches in 18K white gold. Each set with 456 pink, white or yellow diamonds.

"I enjoyed visiting Russia while I developed the concept

ABOVE
Ladies' watch in 18K white, yellow and rose gold set with 148 brilliants (16.83 carats), made of 14 flowers set with 13 yellow brilliants (3.57 carats) and 87 marquise-cut diamonds in different colors (11.32 carats).

for the Pushkin collection, because at the time, the Russians were enjoying the sophistication and glitter of society and cultural events," says Scheufele.

As her collections continue to experience phenomenal success, Caroline Gruosi-Scheufele turns her sights toward business development. Her goal is to have Chopard boutiques in major cities all around the world in order to maintain close association with the public. "We are known as a creative company and I would like to preserve that, as well as the exclusive quality of our jewelry."

RIGHT
Ring in 18K white and yellow gold set with white and yellow diamonds (respectively 1.55 carats and 1.70 carats), a heart-shaped white diamond (1.22 carats) and a heart-shaped yellow diamond (1.15 carats).

Roberto Coin

The imagination of Roberto Coin pushes constantly forward, moving in perfect unison with the changing world around us. Each new Roberto Coin collection is anticipated with the greatest curiosity, but also with the certain knowledge that all of his designs are sure to be original in their style and striking in their beauty.

LEFT AND BELOW
Appassionata ring and earrings in 18K yellow gold.

FACING PAGE
Appassionata bracelets, in 18K white, yellow gold, with diamonds.

Twenty years ago, Coin made three-color gold fashionable. He was the first to work in high-quality two-color gold, and brought back into fashion satin and silk finish in jewelry. In the past five years, Coin has created a new collection in white gold that has already been recognized as a classic.

Roberto Coin has an extensive clientele in Europe, the United States, South America and the Far East. Every year Coin produces more than 600 models of high-quality jewelry. A team of highly skilled workers uses time-honored techniques in concert with modern innovations to guarantee that each piece is of exceptional quality.

Appassionata is the name of Coin's newest collection, in which the designer has outdone himself once again. It is more than just a new line of jewelry; it is an advancement in technology that succeeds in combining skill with cre-

TOP
Bracelet in 18K white gold with diamonds.
CENTER
Roberto Coin
LEFT
Bangle in 18K white gold and diamonds.

ABOVE
Animalia bangles in 18K yellow gold.

LEFT
Rings in 18K gold with natural colored stones and diamonds.

ativity to produce exquisite results. Appassionata is a new experience in wearing gold. The gold is woven together in such a way that it flows in one continuous stream and feels as supple as a piece of cloth. It took two years for Coin and his master craftsmen to perfect this method, which has now been patented. To further increase the delight one takes in wearing this exclusive design, there is a marquise ruby set on the inside of the gold. According to ancient Egyptian legend, a ruby touching the skin brings happiness and good fortune. For this reason, the ruby is Coin's favorite gem. Of course, the designer always falls in love with his creations and is particularly excited with his latest, the Appassionata collection.

ABOVE
Parisian weave collection in yellow, white and rose gold.

BOTTOM
Bangle from the 365 collection, in 18K gold with diamonds.

FACING PAGE ABOVE
Hugs and Kisses collection by Isabella Iannicelli in 18K white gold with diamonds.

FACING PAGE BELOW
Nabucco Collection bracelets in 18K yellow and white gold with diamonds and natural colored stones.

Roberto Coin has devoted himself to designing and creating since he was a child. Pursuing this love, in 1976 he established himself as a jeweler. The other members of the Coin family are also intimately involved in jewelry-making: Roberto's wife is a qualified gemologist, and their son is responsible for the administration of the business.

The inspiration for every piece of Roberto Coin jewelry is entirely personal, but the designer does keep an eye on trends in the fashion industry. For instance, when fashion designers began using more black and shades of gray, Coin turned to white gold and white gold with diamonds — perfect complements to the darker tones of contemporary couture.

Roberto Coin adheres to a belief that every jewel a woman wears should be an expression of her own individuality. Each of his pieces of fine jewelry is crafted to satisfy this philosophy, as is apparent in Coin's newest collections: Nabucco, 365 and, of course, Appassionata. The intricacies of a Roberto Coin design stem from his love of a challenge, and his insistence that each design stimulate both the mind and the senses. The results are fascinating and always appealing.

de Grisogono

A SERPENT SLITHERS AROUND THE NECK, its skin gleaming in shiny black and white diamonds.... Golden frogs ready to pounce into an emerald pool 30 carats deep.... A fan flutters in the wind, with yellow diamonds and gold flickering in the sun. This fantastic dreamland, unexpected in the landscape of Haute Joaillerie, is the invention of designer Fawaz Gruosi, owner of de Grisogono jeweler. As Gruosi sketches whimsical designs in the studio of his boutique in Geneva, he allows no stone to take precedence over his imagination, no matter the size, color or value. Fawaz Gruosi is enchanted with capturing what others have not even anticipated, and he does not heed convention. While precious gems inspire and command attention, in the de Grisogono collection, fantasy and dreams prevail.

LEFT
Earrings in yellow and white gold, set with four spectacular Colombian emeralds (61 carats), black and white diamonds.

FACING PAGE
Sumptuous necklace in yellow and white gold set with 80 carats of black diamonds, 23.9 carats of white diamonds, enhanced by 11 spectacular Colombian emeralds (189.57 carats.)

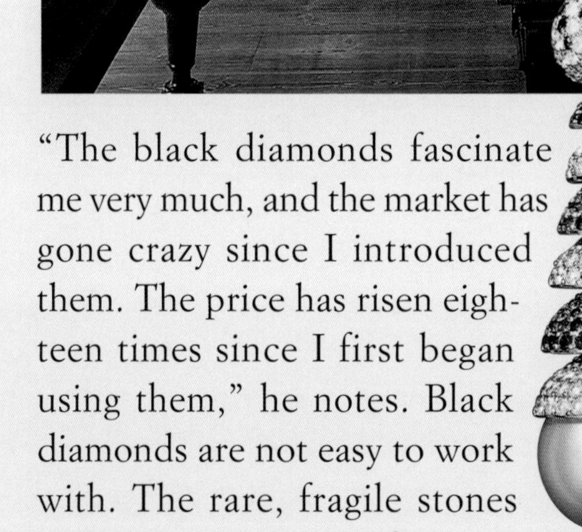

A provocateur in the world of jewelry, Fawaz Gruosi ushered in the use of the now popular black diamond, but this idea initially raised eyebrows. "They thought I was crazy. They said there is no life in the black diamond," recalls Fawaz Gruosi. "But as you can see, they have a lot of luster and have their own life within themselves, just like all natural colored diamonds." As the modern discoverer of the stone — the black gems made a rare appearance during the Art Deco period in the 1930s — Fawaz Gruosi has developed his own grading system: grey, grey black and jet black, which he ranks as the equivalent to a d-flawless white diamond.

"The black diamonds fascinate me very much, and the market has gone crazy since I introduced them. The price has risen eighteen times since I first began using them," he notes. Black diamonds are not easy to work with. The rare, fragile stones often crumble during cutting. Black, being a neutral color, offers an extraordinary contrast when combined with other gemstones. "They simply become irresistible. Black is beautiful and romantic," he says.

CLOCKWISE FROM FAR LEFT
Black Diamonds collection heart pendant. Sketch of Black Diamonds collection. Superb "Chandelier" earrings set with diamonds weighing 57 carats, limited design of five pairs. Interior of de Grisogono boutique in Geneva. Earrings with South Sea pearls pendants, sparkling with emeralds, sapphires and diamonds. Fawaz Gruosi, designer and owner of de Grisogono.

ABOVE
"Hearts" necklace in white gold set with 33.60 carats of white diamonds and 60.42 carats of black diamonds.

LEFT
Exceptional ring in white gold whose 12.5 carats of black diamonds are set around a magnificent 7 carat emerald-cut white diamond.

BELOW
Sketches for a model. Yellow gold ring set with a white pearl and 8.47 carats of black diamonds.

Among his stunning and exclusive Black Diamonds collection is a delicate "Chandelier" earring of cascading black and white diamonds. Set in an unusual open setting that allows space between the gem and gold, the multi-faceted black diamonds shimmer as brightly as the white diamonds. In another piece, a black-and-white diamond spotted terrier looks dashing in his blue sapphire collar. Mirroring the full eclipse of the moon, a pair of heart-shaped earrings are the converse of one another: on one earring, a black diamond pavé heart rests on a white diamond pavé heart, and on the other, a white diamond pavé heart rests on a black diamond pavé heart.

BELOW
Pair of original heart-shaped white gold earrings featuring about 17 carats of black diamonds and 13.50 carats of white diamonds.

A relative newcomer to the domain of designing, Fawaz Gruosi has spent

ABOVE
"Zebra set" necklace and earrings set with black and white diamonds.

RIGHT
Pendant earrings featuring white gold spheres pavéed with 27.71 carats of black diamonds and enhanced with white diamonds weighing 2.31 carats.

LEFT
Exceptional white gold ring set with a pear-cut black diamond of approximately 32 carats, pavéed with 21 carats of Burmese rubies and white diamonds weighing about 1 carat.

BOTTOM LEFT AND RIGHT
The de Grisogono boutique in Geneva. "Terrier" brooch set with white and black diamonds and sapphires.

his life immersed in the jewelry profession. Married to Caroline Scheufele, jewelry designer and vice-president of Chopard, Fawaz Gruosi also creates items for Chopard, such as the stunning "Ice Cube" watch and the "Casmir" timepiece, featuring a watchface of a solitary paisley drop, covered in diamonds. Black diamonds circle a ring, only to be punctuated with circles of white diamonds in extraordinary settings that seem otherworldly. Romance figures in his "You and I" set of rings, in which two diamond rings harmonize perfectly: a white diamond pavé ring holds a one-carat black diamond in the center; its mate is a black diamond pavé ring with a one-carat white diamond in the center.

"I'm in love with my work. I'm always trying to make my creations a provocation," he says, referring to an eye-popping emerald that he's surrounded with a setting

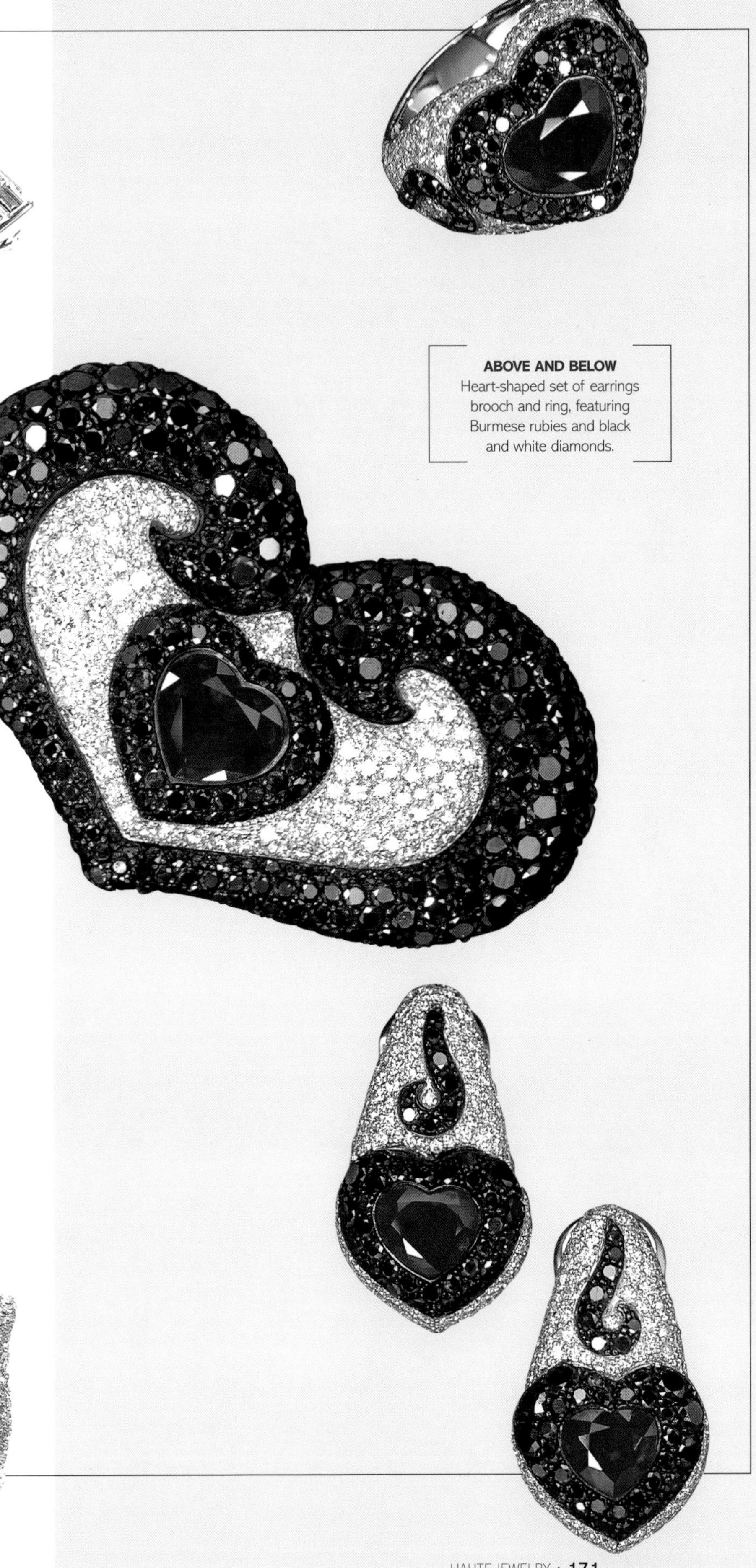

ABOVE AND BELOW
Heart-shaped set of earrings brooch and ring, featuring Burmese rubies and black and white diamonds.

RIGHT
Ring in yellow gold featuring an 11-carat emerald-cut diamond encircled by baguette-cut emeralds and an 8-carat emerald encircled by baguette-cut diamonds.

BELOW
This one-of-a-kind "Frog" ring in yellow gold is set with a Colombian emerald weighing about 30 carats and features three claws set with emeralds and jonquil diamonds, the fourth enhanced with jonquil diamonds.

incorporating frogs and lily pads when such a large stone traditionally would be set as a solitaire. "What I'm referring to is a piece that gives someone the opportunity to say, 'This guy is crazy.'" This daring designer is also one of the only jewelers to use brown and grey cabochon diamonds, which look rather like tiger's eye pearls, if there were such things.

Fawaz Gruosi founded de Grisogono in 1994 with two partners whom he soon bought out. In just four years, he has already expanded to open a second jewelry boutique in Burlington Gardens, London. As owner, he selects the stones, designs the pieces and is also in charge of sales. The boutique on Rue de Rhône in Geneva boasts a collection of selected antiques that fulfill perfectly his vision of fantasy. The showroom is an eclectic, elegant and inviting space that instantly transports clients into that fabled realm where dreams come true in the most unexpected ways....

RIGHT
One-of-a-kind yellow gold ring set with a Colombian emerald weighing about 15 carats and pavéed with white and pink diamonds.

Martin Gruber

In the remarkable jewelry of Martin Gruber, the diamond plays the role both of centerpiece and essential design element. Well known for his innovative settings for diamonds, Gruber also incorporates the precious gems into the entire construction of each piece, and the result is jewels of multiple dimension that sparkle from every angle. A trendsetter in the world of jewelry, Martin Gruber possesses a particularly incisive understanding of the different feeling expressed by each cut of diamond. In one award-winning design, baguette diamonds stand upright in a futuristic style. In another, the diamonds are set in such a fashion that they look like a laser beam. Each creation is on the cutting edge of design; that is, until Gruber reveals his next vision.

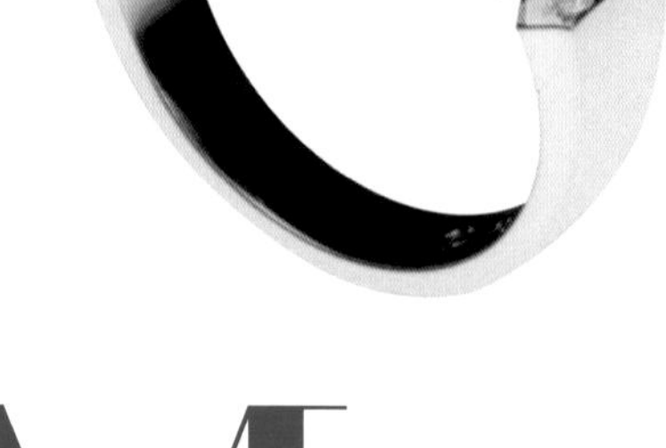

LEFT
The award winning "Sawtooth" ring from 1974, with 24 brilliant-cut diamonds weighing 1.07 carats and a 2-carat brilliant center.

FACING PAGE
One-of-a-kind, one-million-dollar belt has 1.45 pounds of 18K gold housing 91 pear-shaped diamonds that weigh a total of 154.29 carats.

FAR LEFT CLOCKWISE FROM TOP LEFT
A small sample of Martin Gruber's Mystery collection: Three-row gradual "Mystery" band with 28 princess- and baguette-cut diamonds totaling 2.87 carats. "Invisible Slope" semi-mount 11 princess- and baguette-cut diamond trilor weighing .83 carats with a .75-carat brilliant center. "Mystery" favorite band with 12 baguette-cut diamonds, 10 princess-cut sapphires and one diamond trilor weighing approx. 2.5 carats. "Mystery" baguette/PC Anniversary band with alternating princess- and baguette-cut diamonds weighing 1.82 carats. Three-row "Mystery" bracelet with 199 princess- and baguette-cut diamonds weighing 21.77 carats. "Mystery Golden Gate" semi-mount diamond ring with 37 princess- and baguette-cut diamonds weighing 1.77 carats and a 3.42-carat canary yellow emerald-cut diamond center stone. "AMIAMIAMI" semimount diamond ring has 23 princess- and baguette-cut diamonds totaling 1.63 carats and a 3-carat brilliant center.

TOP RIGHT
Sketch for the appropriately named "Award Winning" diamond ring featuring 76 set baguette diamonds weighing 4.5 carats.

Born into a family of jewelers, Gruber assumed control of the family business in 1971, and, following in his father's footsteps, set out to develop high-quality, innovative jewelry. "My father didn't know how to make something cheaply," Gruber recalls. "And I can't create pieces that seem unfinished. A jewel, through design, should be transformed into something new, something that has never before been seen."

LEFT ABOVE
Martin Gruber on one of his BMW motorbikes in California.

LEFT BELOW
"Nugget" watch band designed and developed by Martin Gruber in 1968 helped put Nova on the map.

In the late 1960s into the early '70s, Gruber invented a style of jewelry that would define the next two decades. "During this time, there was a big oil rush in Texas, and newfound millionaires celebrated their wealth by rewarding themselves with gold. Every Texas oil man was wearing a Rolex and a big gold bracelet with diamonds," explains Gruber. At the same time, "free-form" jewelry was popular, and Gruber began his own explorations within that realm. It was during this time that he created Nugget jewelry, made of random, irregular shapes of gold. An instant success, the design became enormously popular and appeared in a variety of new forms, from rings to pendants to watch bracelets.

Soon after, Martin Gruber began experimenting with the use of diamonds, forever changing the way the brilliant and fiery gems would be viewed. His first revolutionary and award-winning design features diamonds floating amidst golden supports. Known as the Sawtooth setting, Gruber created it in 1974 for a specific competition at a time when most jewelry was either prong- or bezel-set. "We built a tradition of winning contests," Gruber says. At his company headquarters, Nova Jewelry in Van Nuys, California, two hallways are lined with thirty awards honoring Gruber for his creativity, including three DeBeers "Diamond International" awards.

Inspired by the initial honor for the Sawtooth setting, Gruber set out to further explore new dimensions in design. In 1975, he developed the striking and innovative Heartribs curved channel setting. Countless designs followed, including a limited edition ring created in 1982 that featured baguettes, so that "everywhere you look, you see diamonds," says Gruber.

In 1985, his designs showcased the rarely used baguette-cut diamonds in a gravity-defying effect. The baguettes stand upright, creating a subtle, architectural style. "The baguette-cut is like a mirror, it doesn't have the refractive qualities of a

ABOVE
CLOCKWISE FROM TOP
"Paradis" with 45 invisible-set baguetttes weighing 3.09 carats and a brilliant center of 3 carats. "Magnifique" with 65 princess- and baguette-cut diamonds weighing 6.46 carats surrounding the 3.3-carat marquise center stone. "The Diamond Splendour" has 69 princess-cut diamonds with baguettes weighing 2.17 carats and a 2.5-carat brilliant-cut center. "Ice on Fire" with 45 princess- and baguette-cut diamonds weighing 2.97 carats surrounding the 2.5-carat diamond center stone. "Assymetrical Balance" semi-mount diamond ring has 36 princess- and baguette-cut diamonds weighing 2.24 carats and a 3-carat princess-cut diamond at the center.

RIGHT
This necklace has 220 diamonds weighing 30.99 carats with a 23.95-carat diamond center.

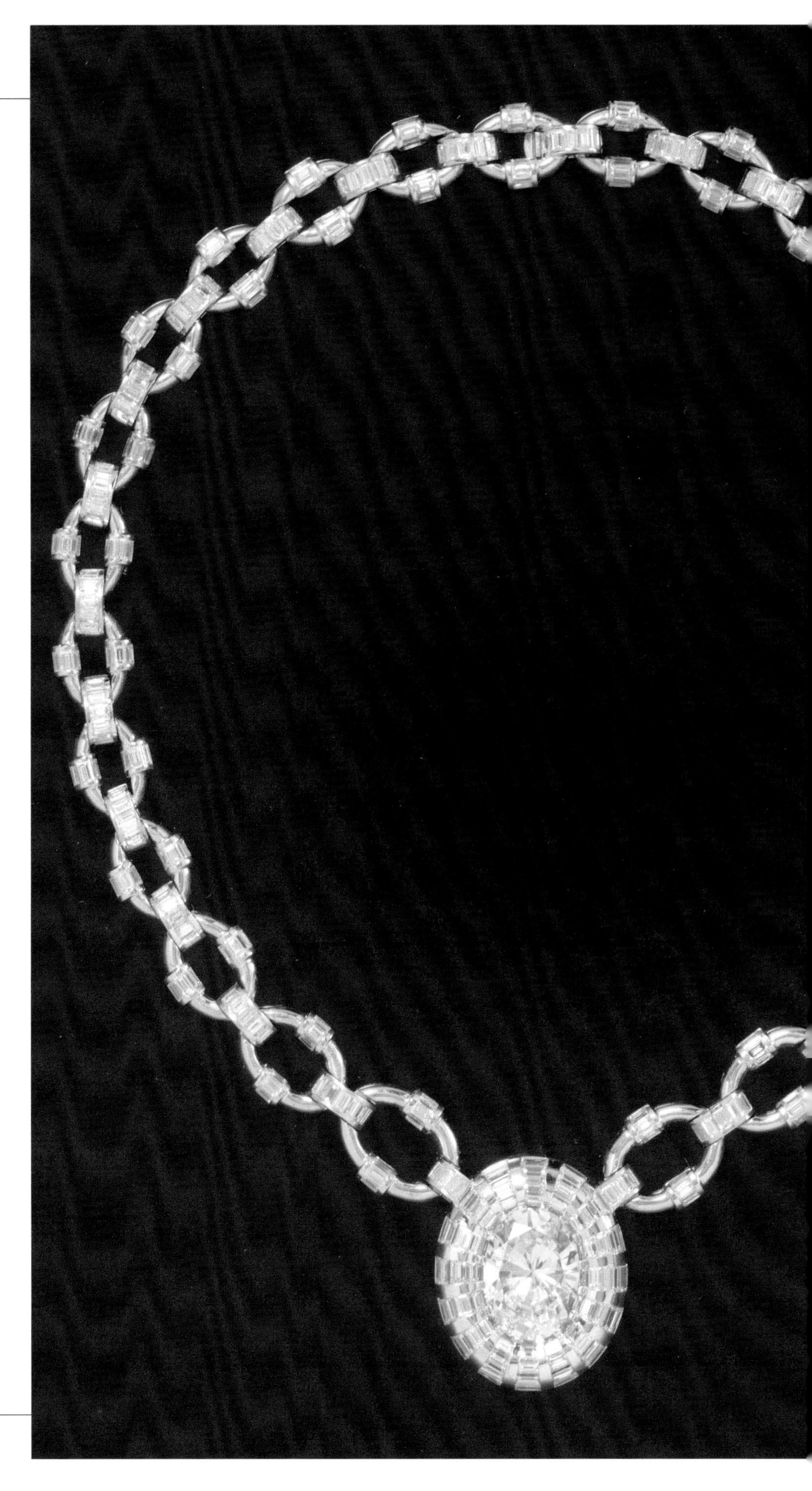

round stone, yet it's more subtle, which reflects my design philosophy of 'less is more.'"

Gruber's explorations ultimately launched several definitive collections, including the Mystery, Fantasy, Golden Gate, Strands and Odyssey lines. A true artist, Gruber sees inspiration everywhere, as with his homage to San Francisco's famous Golden Gate Bridge. His creations also evoke a unique sense of imagination: The Odyssey line captures the image of a laser beam, while the Strands collection introduces a new application of gold, using thin strands to encase diamonds in an eye-catching geometrical pattern. "To me, round stones are like ornamentation, baguettes are like girders, and together they made the mosaic whole, creating a perfect balance," he explains.

"I could never produce all of the things I am inspired to design," says Gruber. "The designing part of it doesn't take that much time, I just seem to have an endless source of inspiration." No doubt that is one of the chief reasons that his jewelry business is so successful; even more significantly, his success seems to stem from the joy Gruber finds in his work. "It's very gratifying that people get pleasure out of what I do — but I'm already happy, so long as I'm creating new jewelry."

TOP LEFT CLOCKWISE FROM FAR LEFT
"Invisible Slope" semi-mount has 11 diamonds weighing .83 carats with a 2.5-carat pear shape center. "Mystery Golden Gate." houses 37 diamonds weighing 1.66 carats, and has a 3.25-carat emerald center. "The Diamond Splendour" has 69 diamonds weighing 2.17 carats with a 2.5-carat brilliant center. "Paradis" with invisible-set baguettes weighing 3.09 carats with a brilliant center of 3 carats. "Magnifique" has diamonds weighing 6.46 carats which surround the 3.3-carat marquise center. "7-Row Princess-Cut Baguette Reflection" bracelet has 521 diamonds weighing 19.79 carats. "Double Fantasy" diamond band, a striking example of Martin's award-winning designs, has 45 diamonds weighing 4.91 carats. Pair of "Crossover Fantasy" earrings crafted with 119 diamonds weighing 6.88 carats.

TOP RIGHT
"Crossover Fantasy" has 44 invisibly set princess-cut diamonds and 38 standing baguettes for a total weight of 3.22 carats.

CENTER LEFT
The "Vatche" diamond ring with 66 diamonds totalling 4.73 carats.

BOTTOM LEFT
"Stepping Across" invisibly set diamond band has 46 diamonds weighing 2.51 carats.

FACING PAGE
The necklace consists of 300 emerald-cut and baguette diamonds weighing 47.96 carats. The fancy yellow diamond center stone weighs 15.22 carats. The emerald-cut baguette ring has 16 diamonds weighing 3.20 carats with a fancy yellow diamond center that weighs 7.87 carats. The earrings feature a total of 106 diamonds weighing 26.75 carats with fancy yellow diamond centerpieces weighing 9.22 and 9.37 carats. The emerald-cut baguette bracelet has 109 diamonds weighing 18.39 carats.

Lalaounis

In a century filled with remarkable jewelry and jewelry makers, Ilias Lalaounis impresses with one of the most fascinating careers of all. Acknowledged as an unsurpassed master in the use of gold, the Greek jeweler has also had a powerful and permanent influence on international jewelry design in a myriad of directions. For example, the renaissance of a substantial number of ancient artistic traditions is owed in large part to the work of Lalaounis. Almost incredibly, Lalaounis has also created some of the most significant avant-garde jewelry — sometimes abstract, often scientifically based — that has Lalaounis began his exploration of ancient methods as a young jeweler after two women asked that whether he could reproduce two Mycenaean brooches they had seen in the archeological museum. Drawn to the rich history of the artifacts, Lalaounis dedicated himself to studying ancient civilizations and the techniques that yielded magnificent jewels.

ABOVE
Bracelet in 18K gold inspired by the Shield fresco at the Palace of Knossos.

FACING PAGE
Necklace and earrings in 18K gold in the form of rows of stylised papyrus flowers. Glass, gold, or clay beads in that shape are often found in Minoan and Mycenean graves.

COUNTERCLOCKWISE
Ioanna, Demetra, Katerini, and Maria Lalounis;

Ilias Lalaounis at the Académie des Beaux Arts in Paris, during his investiture ceremony;

Ilias and Lila Lalaounis at the ancient Theater of Dionysos in Athens;

Necklace in 18K gold and rock crystal. The main theme is a design from a "krateftis" of the late Neolithic (4th millenium BC) found at Sesklo, Central Greece;

Neogeometric Collection (1973). Bracelet in 18K gold wire designed by means of computer graphics.

Lalaounis' historical focus has led to his concentration on gold as the central element of his jewelry, and the success of his creations has played a major part in the revival of the art of goldsmithing in his native country. His most famous designs — drawing on the patterns and motifs of classical Greek art — have been internationally emulated.

While Lalaounis frequently returns to the inspirational wellspring of his native culture, his interest in the artistry of ancient civilizations spans the globe. For instance, although gold may well be Lalaounis' signature, the appeal of Byzantine visual design — and its famed extravagance — has led him to produce a wide range of exciting work involving precious and semiprecious stones. Generating ideas from many sources, Lalaounis draws from the architecture as well as the beautiful mosaics of the Byzantine era, resulting in jewelry of intricate construction and often astonishing color.

In addition to the classic styles of the Hellenistic and Byzantine eras, Lalaounis has also worked in motifs from the Neolithic, Cycladic and Minoan eras. The fascination that bygone civilizations hold for Lalaounis has led him even further afield in his pursuit of ancient techniques and styles. Lalaounis established his mastery of Persian art with the collection he presented to Farah Diba, widow of the late Shah of Iran.

Lalaounis has also created collections to celebrate the opening of his boutiques in countries around the

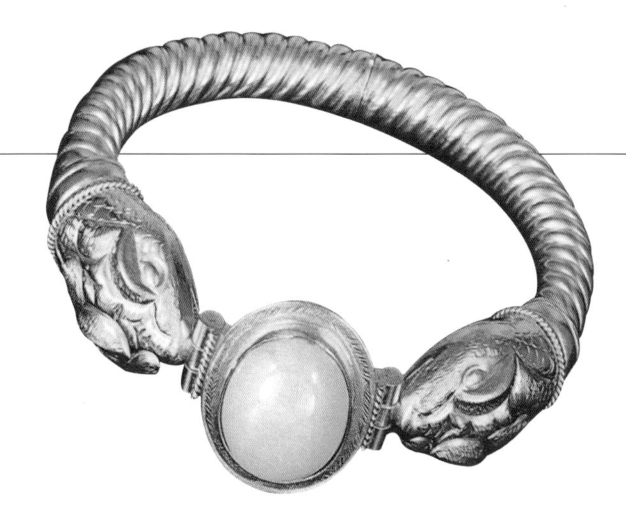

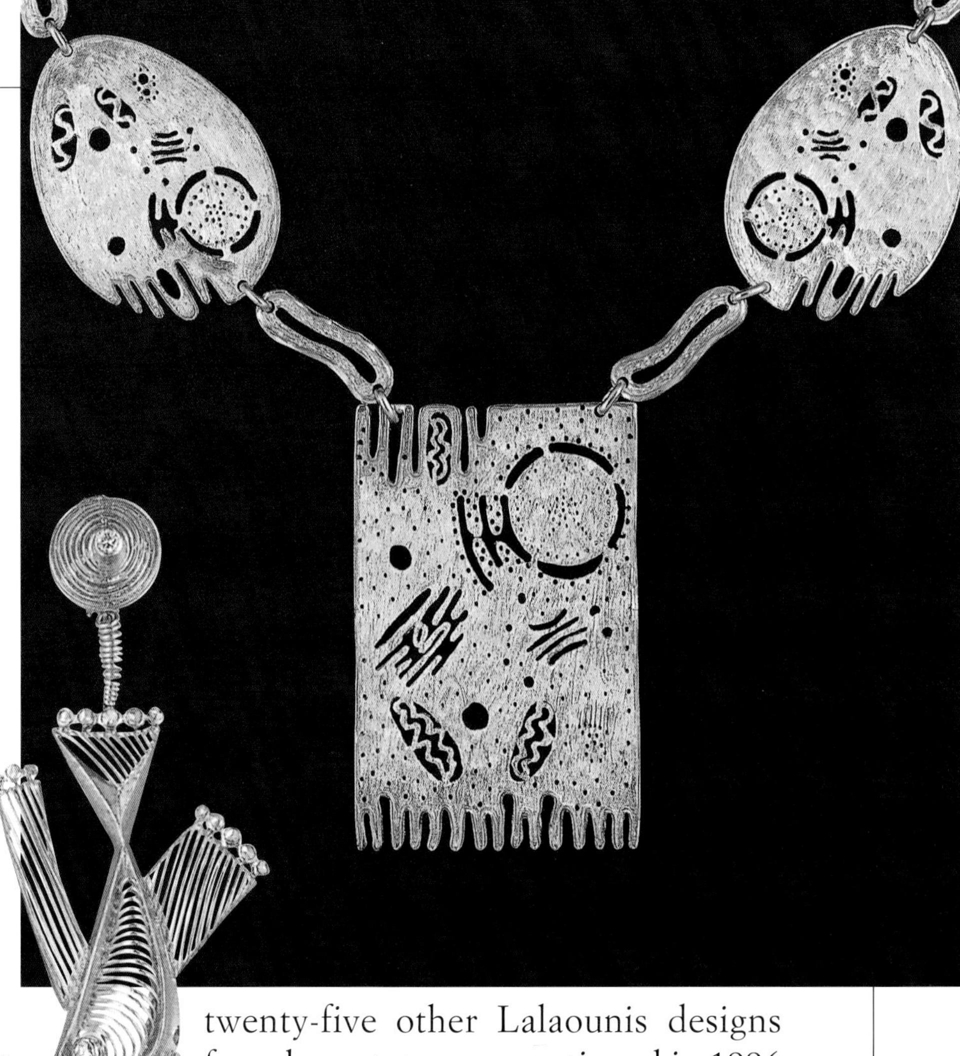

world. For Japan there was the Far East collection; for England, the Tudor and the Celtic collections; and for the United States, the Amerindian collection.

One of Lalaounis' most unusual collections was inspired by the works attributed to the ancient Scythians of Central and Southern Russia. From this remarkable series — and fifteen other Lalaounis collections — a total of 300 pieces were chosen for an exhibition celebrating the 100th anniversary of the Pushkin Museum of Moscow. This was the first time that the work of a contemporary Greek jeweler was displayed in a Russian museum.

TOP LEFT
Bracelet in 20-22K twisted gold with two snakes' heads clasping a turquoise medallion between their fangs.

TOP RIGHT
Biosymbols Collection (1972). Necklace in 18K gold reproducing the microstructure of a human cell.

CENTER
Pair of earrings in 18K gold and diamonds in the form of stylised fish. The design recalls drawings on Minoan pots, with studies of sealife.

Lalaounis has established an international reputation of great distinction over the years. One of his more celebrated champions was Aristotle Onassis, who commissioned Lalaounis to create a pair of earrings for Jacqueline Kennedy Onassis. These and twenty-five other Lalaounis designs from her estate were auctioned in 1996 at Sotheby's in New York. With many important designs to his name, Lalaounis has been recognized not only as one of the world's great jewelers, but as a fine artist as well. In 1990, he was the first jeweler to be inducted into the Academie des Beaux Arts of the Institut de France.

Contemporary life also provides Lalaounis with inspiration and his jewelry explores the beauty of scientific and technological breakthroughs.Under Lalaounis' gaze elements of the human body, explored through the use of microscopic and com-

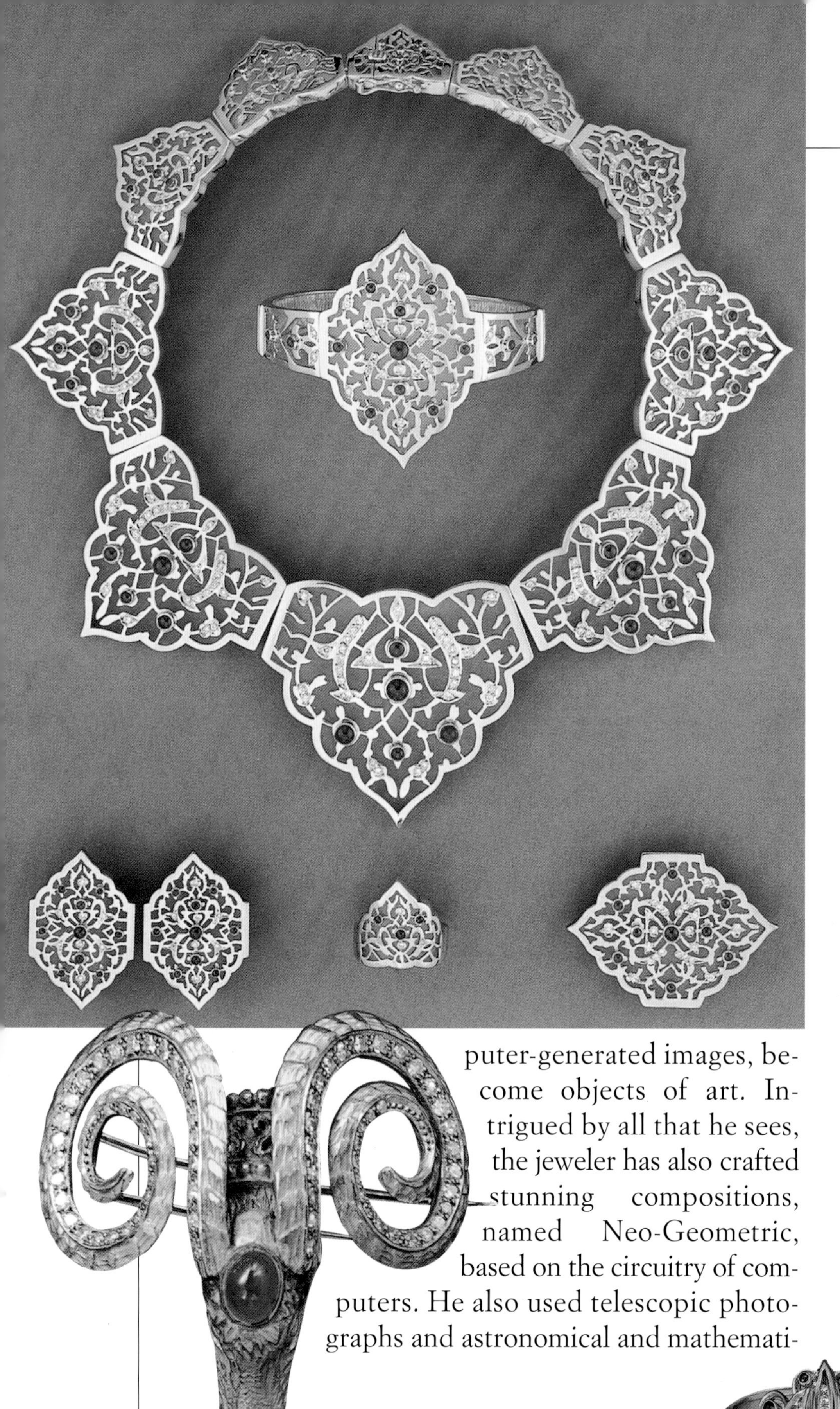

puter-generated images, become objects of art. Intrigued by all that he sees, the jeweler has also crafted stunning compositions, named Neo-Geometric, based on the circuitry of computers. He also used telescopic photographs and astronomical and mathematical drawings for his Motion in Space collection.

Ilias' four daughters are now intimately involved in the running of the family enterprise. Each works in a different area of the business, and all are as dedicated to it as their father. In 1994, the entire family participated in the opening of the Ilias Lalaounis Jewelry Museum, which displays 3000 pieces from the designer's forty-five collections to date. Appropriately, the museum is housed in Lalaounis' original workshop situated across from the Acropolis. Its exhibits ensure that the great works of Lalaounis will continue to enjoy their richly deserved acclaim.cal drawings for his Motion in

TOP LEFT
Suleyman the Magnificent (1988). Set of necklace, bracelet, brooch, earrings, and finger ring in 18K gold, rock crystal and rubies. The gold decoration follows patterns in illuminated manuscripts of the Ottoman period.

TOP RIGHT
Finger rings in rock crystal and obsidian with 18K gold and precious stones based on 16th century archer's thumb rings.

LOWER LEFT
Ram's head brooch in 18K gold, diamonds and a cabochon ruby. The ram, symbol of prosperity, was another favorite subject of Classical Greek Art.

LOWER RIGHT
Bracelet in 18K gold with rubies, sapphires and diamonds, influenced by Byzantine decorative motifs.

FACING PAGE
Necklace in 18K gold in the technique of the mosaic. It is studded with rubies, sapphires and emeralds, similar to Byzantine jewelry.

Doris Panos

ENRICHED BY THE INFLUENCES OF HER HERITAGE, jewelry designer Doris Panos has taken the flavor of her Byzantine and Greek roots and created a collection that adheres to traditional ties while suiting today's lifestyles. For generations, her family has enjoyed the art of jewelry making, and it was inevitable that Doris would begin exploring her inherent artistry. A unique combination of established tradition and personal passion drove Doris to pursue the individuality of her spirit and to create a collection that has opened up a new era for today's jewelry.

ABOVE
18K white gold handmade ring with 13-carat oval blue-green tourmaline accented with diamonds.

FACING PAGE
Doris is wearing an 18K white gold "Belladonna" necklace with black pearls and diamonds. She is also wearing a black South Sea pearl "pillow" ring with diamond hoops and detachable South Sea pearl drops. Stackable bangles feature pearl pagoda and portofino bracelets.

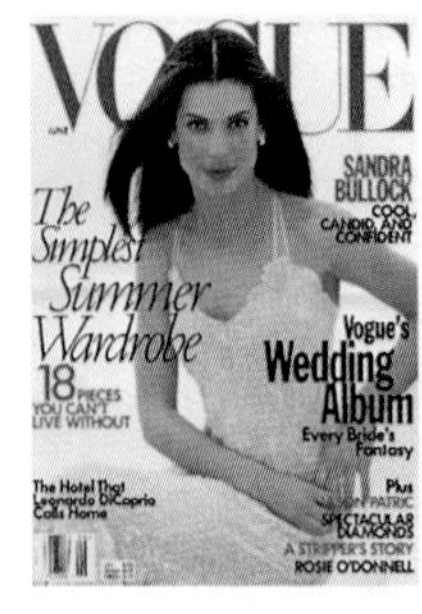

After studying business administration and art in college, Doris amassed seventeen years of experience in the jewelry industry—ranging from manufacturing to the colored stone and diamond business to working one-on-one with clients at prestigious Fifth Avenue retail establishments—all of which led her to successfully launch her own collection. Lauded with the highest of honors, her designs were consecutively awarded and praised by the Women's Jewelry Association, American Gem Trade Association and Jewelers of America. Doris credits her success to "a combination of my apprenticeships and constant feedback from clients that wear my designs."

Doris breaks down the barriers of conformity and creates jewelry that is sophisticated and unique. Her contemporary designs reveal classicism in an exceptional harmony of modern and traditional style. A refined 18-karat matte gold collection boasts the versatility of stackable designs in which a woman may wear three, two, or just one jewelry item, providing a variety of looks for any mood. By revolutionizing the art of stacking jewelry and reinvigorating the use of matte gold, Doris has built a tremendous following.

Doris' many collections, which include

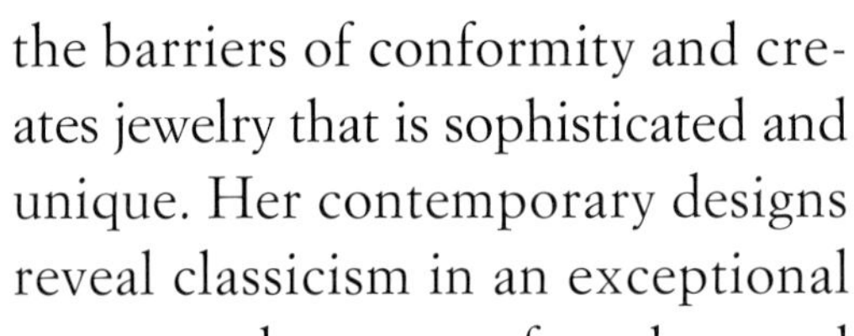

CLOCKWISE FROM ABOVE CENTER
18K white gold "Zoie" ring and "Classico" remount.
18K white gold "Fig Leaf" and "Orchid" pins from the "Back to Nature" collection adorned with diamonds and South Sea pearls.
18K white gold stackable bands from the "Ecstasy" collection.

"Romance" and "Ecstasy," all evoke the eternal theme of romance and woman's seductive power. Doris amplifies this feminine magic by contrasting different metals with diamonds and precious stones to accommodate the unpredictable personalities of each woman. Capitalizing on the impact of her jewelry, Doris has emerged as a purveyor of sensuality.

THIS PAGE
18K white gold "Monaco" collection.

Renowned for its mass appeal, the latest "Back to Nature" brooch collection embraces the whims of sophisticated women who enjoy elegantly accessorizing their business suits. Adorned with diamonds and South Sea pearls, the various motifs include mushrooms, acorns, fig leafs, orchid and clovers. With its deco appeal, the "Monaco" collection has received rave reviews for its unique styling and contemporary flair.

Doris travels throughout America and the Caribbean to make countless personal appearances and to visit with her fiercely loyal clientele. The empire behind Doris is attributed

LEFT
Doris wears a complete set of her 18K white gold "Clover" collection.
RIGHT
18K gold stackable bangles from the "Clover" collection.
BELOW LEFT
18K white gold "Ecstasy" collection.
BELOW RIGHT
18K "Romance" and "Passion" bands..

not only to the superiority of her designs and craftsmanship, but also to her effusive charm—clients adore her for her wit and honesty.

Doris takes pride in her masterpiece jewelry and the accolades she has won, yet she does not allow fame to keep her from her obligations. Doris is an advocate for a number of charities, participating in fundraisers that assist medical advances, including cancer-related research. As a wife and mother of two, Doris is deeply committed to family-related issues.

In recent years, various books and magazines have celebrated Doris' many achievements and her relentless drive to create incomparable jewelry. Doris' image has graced the covers of every major fashion magazine — always keen to the statement of the moment, she never fails to realize that stylish jewelry doesn't necessarily have to be trendy.

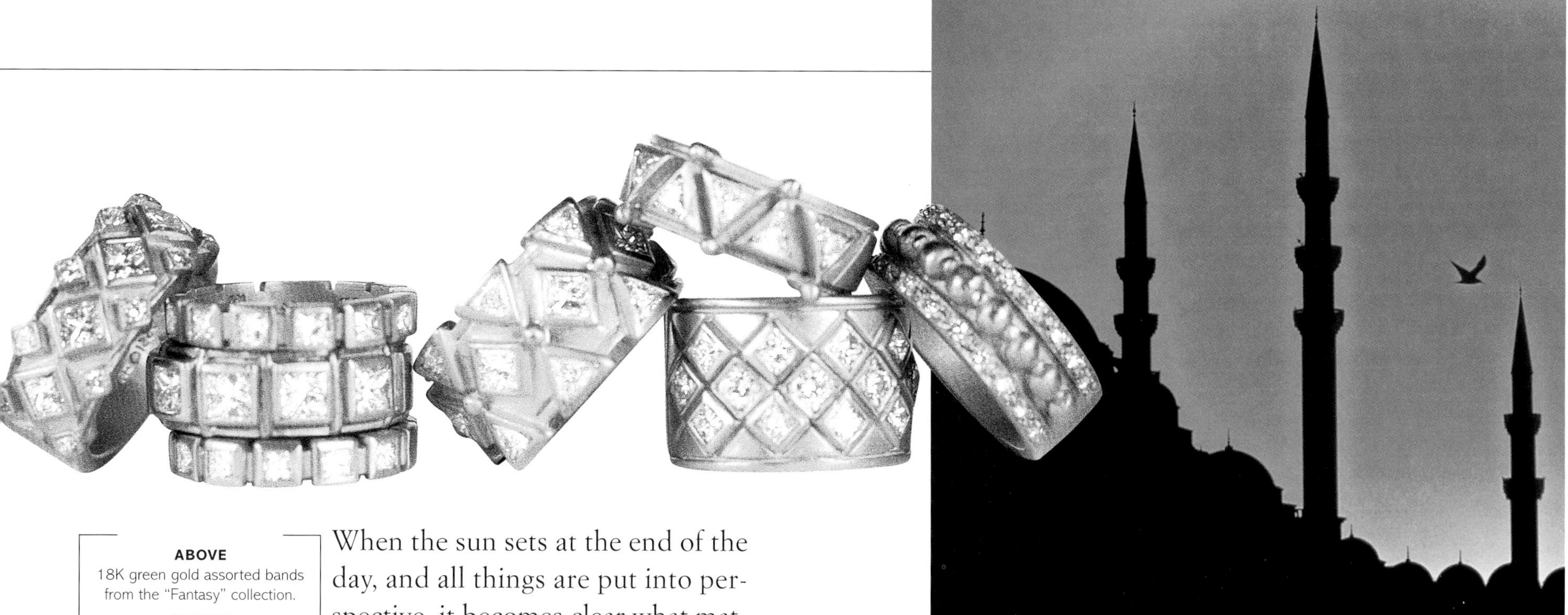

ABOVE
18K green gold assorted bands from the "Fantasy" collection.
BELOW
18K white and green gold stackable bangles and bands from the "Romance" collection.

When the sun sets at the end of the day, and all things are put into perspective, it becomes clear what matters to Doris the most: "The reaction that one has after wearing my jewelry. To me, there is no greater satisfaction, and that makes all the hard work and endless efforts worthwhile."

With her successful, well-established company running smoothly, Doris has a tremendous impact on younger clientele who look up to her, and older clientele that appreciate her perseverance in creating sumptuous designs. Her collection appeals to many generations and embraces a timeless fashion, an achievement of which Doris is proud. Only thirty-five years old, she has accomplished in five years what has taken many of her peers twenty or more. It is evident that Doris will continue to make impressive strides and will no doubt continue to be recognized as a remarkably young and powerful force in the industry. For those who have an insatiable desire for the finest of jewelry, there will always be unique, irresistible Panos jewelry to enjoy.

Piranesi

IN LIFE, EXCELLENCE IS NEVER AN ACCIDENT. At Piranesi, a world leader in the design and craftsmanship of fine jewelry, its founders and their heirs have worked tirelessly to deliver such uncompromising excellence for over a century. Established in 1845 in Valenza, Italy, Piranesi has been providing its respected clientele with unparalleled service and jewelry for several generations. Leaders in the world of colored stones, the House of Piranesi also aims to create fashionable jewelry designed for living. Through its finely crafted collections, Piranesi pursues a dual goal — to create comfort coupled with the confidence that their discreetly elegant jewelry exemplifies. Its current collections reflect a most discreet and revered jewelry house as it prepares to continue its legacy into the next century.

LEFT
Double pear-shaped diamond earrings in 18K white gold.

FACING PAGE
An important South Sea pearl and diamond parure. The line of nine white button pearls highlight the circular-cut and marquise-cut diamond necklace which also supports a delicate fringe of nine silver-colored South Sea pearl drops. These pearls, which are slightly graduated in size, are topped by circular-cut diamond caps and mounted in 18K white gold. The matching earrings, with three hanging silver South Sea pearls from each earring, are mounted in 18K white gold. The top of the earrings are studded with white pearls, framed by round diamonds. The pearl and diamond ring completes the collection. A 13mm South Sea pearl ring embraced by a spiral of pear-, marquise- and round-cut diamonds.

ABOVE
Earrings and matching necklace from the *Sangue Blu* collection in 18K white gold with circular-cut diamonds and oval-cut sapphires.

Piranesi began as a supplier of precious colored stones over a century ago. It quickly became the leading distributor throughout Western and Eastern Europe through its direct relationships with mines worldwide in Colombia, Thailand, Burma, Ceylon and South Africa. During this period, Piranesi also designed magnificent jewelry for royalty the world over. The need to maintain the integrity of its design capabilities led Piranesi to establish its own prestigious jewelry line, launched in 1920. The firm's master Italian jewelers have consistently created classic and contemporary designs revered by connoisseurs internationally. At the end of the twentieth century, the House of Piranesi continues to uphold its historic traditions, rooted in a century long-gone, of craftsmanship, quality and style.

The House of Piranesi built its reputation over the years

ABOVE
A rose pavé-set diamond brooch in 18K pink gold.

LEFT
Pair of heart-shaped earclips from the *Pietra Dura* collection in 18K pink gold with diamonds and heart-shaped mother-of-pearl.

BELOW LEFT AND BELOW
Pietra Dura double-tone 18K pink and brushed white gold earclips contain various designs of hearts which are graduated in size and set with pavé diamonds; matching ring with abstract mother-of-pearl cuts and inlaid diamonds. An example of the *Pietra Dura* collection.

ABOVE
Mesh necklace in 18K white gold interwoven with circular-cut diamonds from the *Sangue Blu* collection. Matching chandelier earrings in 18K white gold with circular-cut diamonds.

BELOW
A splendid parure consisting of necklace and earclips. The necklace's center heart-shaped Colombian emerald is flanked by multiple heart motifs using various cuts of diamonds. The matching earclips are also embellished with Colombian emeralds with hanging hearts studded with diamonds in this stunning example of the *Sangue Blu* collection.

through an uncommon combination of perseverance coupled with obsessive attention to detail. This diligence, however, allowed Piranesi to accomplish what many of today's more impersonal jewelers can never achieve, a truly personal relationship with clientele from around the world. Piranesi's unique intimacy with clients of various cultures contributes to innovative new design ideas and creations for their customers. Rare diamonds, rubies, sapphires and emeralds are the magic ingredients of these prestigious collections that never go out of style. Furthermore, the combination of the family's rich traditions interwoven with contemporary international styling creates a harmony between the past and present. This symmetry of innovation and tradition leaves its unique imprint on all of Piranesi's creations. Through years of diligent care in the making of fine jewelry, Piranesi has been able to maintain the highest standards for its most discerning clientele.

PIETRA DURA COLLECTION

For more than a year, Piranesi's designers sketched as many as 200 ideas before deciding which designs would comprise the spectacular collection named Pietra Dura. It is the result of the jeweler's search for a youthful, fashionable and elegant collection. Refined in diamonds and white gold, or dynamic in colorful precious stones on white or yellow gold, the

line is fashionable for contemporary lifestyles while drawing its mystique from the stones that have enchanted in other times.

ABOVE
A trio of matching coral, milky aquamarine and blue chalcedony rings delicately inlaid with diamonds, part of the *Pietra Dura* collection.

BELOW
Coral and onyx rings with a repeating design and pavé diamonds made of 18K yellow and white gold respectively.

Whether it is the chalcedony made popular by the Duchess of Windsor or the sea-faring talisman aquamarine, behind every precious stone is a love story.

ABOVE LEFT
An artist's sketch from the *Pietra Dura* collection.

ABOVE
Pair of white and pink 18K gold heart pendant chain necklaces from the *Pietra Dura* collection. The repetitive heart patterns of mother-of-pearl and blue agate are elegantly set with diamonds.

LEFT
Pietra Dura parure consists of a necklace and earclips in blue agate embellished with an outline of diamonds embedded in 18K white gold.

Angel's skin, the palest of coral, is the enshrinement of royal passion. Its name first sprung from the lips of Louis XV, who ordained the stone in honor of the beautiful skin of his mistress, Madame de Pompadour. Today, angel's skin of the finest quality is reborn in Piranesi's Pietra Dura collection. Set next to brilliant rubies on a parure with a flower pendant and matching earrings, the necklace reflects the fresh blush of spring.

Piranesi's experts traveled the ends of the world, from Japan to India, Madagascar, Zambia and Egypt for the finest quality crystal rock, jade, mother-of-pearl, turquoise, blue and green agate, as well as angel's skin, chalcedony and aquamarine. Piranesi's designers artfully combine the stones to create a turquoise poodle with diamonds, flowers of chalcedony and blue sapphires, or crystal and rubies for a fascinating summer piece.

COLLEZIONE SANGUE BLU

Jewelry throughout the ages represented an adornment symbolizing rank or wealth. In fact jewelry, which predates clothing, has always been crafted by artisans of the era for those of royalty and wealth. Ancient Egyptians used jewelry with colorful beads and emblematic motifs, such as the scarab. The Greeks enjoyed pure gold ornaments, while Roman jewelry was more massive as ropes of pearls were prized. Medieval jewelry included large brooches and heavy girdles. In the Renaissance, men and women wore gold chains, jeweled collars, and pendants, often designed or even rendered by noted artists. However, during the last century, with factory production and mass reproduction of designs possible, the craft of jewelry artisans has been harder to come by.

Piranesi's new Sangue Blu, or "Blue Blood," collection, is a tribute to the craft practiced for centuries by unnamed artisans and to the royalty that honored the art of jewelry. The collection offers a wide variety of articles differing in style as well as

ABOVE
Parure featuring angel's skin from the *Pietra Dura* collection. The beaded necklace alternates roundels of diamonds, rubies and angel's skin and contains a floral centerpiece. The floral ring and earclips consist of angel's skin petals outlined with diamonds surrounding a ruby cabochon.

CENTER
Pair of diamond-shape cufflinks in 18K gold with coral, onyx and accented by arches of diamonds. An example of the *Pietra Dura* collection.

BOTTOM
Pair of blue agate clover-shaped earclips embellished by circular-cut diamonds, mounted in 18K gold. Part of the *Pietra Dura* collection.

in the materials chosen. The items are born from the hands of an Italian master craftsmen, as if being recreated for the royalty of yesteryear, and the subtle elegance of the collection is readily appreciated. The jewelry whispers a firm affirmation of its wearer's refinement, perfectly balancing grace and substance. The Sangue Blu collection brings- the sensation of softness to the hand and the lightness to the eye. These important pieces radiate the attention to detail brought to their design.

ABOVE AND BELOW
A classical diamond necklace with earrings, in 18K gold. The snowflake motif adds to the necklace's lightness and elegance. Heart drop earrings complete this *Sangue Blu* set.

It may happen that from a single idea a whole series of designs are born, later to be scrutinized for the best fit to the initial concept. However, in the material realization of jewelry today — by machine, in assembly line–style — something is often lost. Unfortunately, the vision of the creation so easily perceived by the artist who imagined, studied and designed the jewelry can be lost due to mass production of jewelry. The Sangue Blu collection preserves the artistic soul of each piece; the original

ABOVE
A splendid parure, consisting of matching necklace, ring, earrings and bracelet with Colombian emerald and various cuts of diamonds, from the *Sangue Blu* collection.

LEFT AND RIGHT
A unique emerald pendant surrounded by various cuts of diamonds supported by a "V" necklace with various cuts of diamonds mounted in platinum. The pendant is detachable and can be worn as a brooch. The earrings consist of two collector's emerald-cut emeralds surrounded by a row of circular-cut diamonds and a second row of pear-shaped diamonds, mounted in platinum and 18K yellow gold.

ABOVE
An 18K white gold and ruby necklace and earrings from the *Sangue Blu* collection, embroidered with graduated oval and pear-shaped rubies. Balancing the rubies are round- and baguette-cut diamonds.

BELOW RIGHT
A brilliant white South Sea pearl necklace constructed in 18K white gold with a paired ring and chandelier earrings are examples of the *Sangue Blu* collection. The diamond embroidery pattern wraps around and balances the pearls.

designer is involved with the entire fabrication process, ensuring that the original idea survives. This is how each piece speaks the same language as that of the artist who contributed to its creation. While the delicate work is apparent, the amount of time Piranesi's artists spend may not be. One may be surprised to learn that more than 150 hours of work are involved in the creation of unique items such as the ones shown on these pages. The time taken to create this piece was devoted not only to design but to the technical work of forging approximately 300 connections between each piece of metal, each of which must be neatly positioned and then hidden behind precious and royal gems. Piranesi's designers strive to design jewelry in much the same spirit of the master craftsmen of centuries before and, as such, Piranesi offers the Sangue Blu collection in honor of royalty and artisans of centuries past.

Roberta

AS EACH SEASON GIVES WAY TO THE NEXT, so too does the passion for a certain gem or item of jewelry. If fashion designers produce new couture collections every season, then shouldn't jewelers create new jewels to add elegance to a spring dress or as a lasting reminder of a bygone summer? While rock crystal and aquamarine set fire to balmy nights, pale yellow and light blue sapphires intimate what spring promises to divulge...

LEFT
Brooch, 18K gold with yellow topaz and diamonds.

FACING PAGE
Bracelet in 18K white gold with blue topaz, yellow topaz, rubies and blue sapphires.

ABOVE
Bracelet in 18K white gold with white crystal and rubies.

ABOVE RIGHT
Roberta Apa Colombo and her two sons.

LEFT
Bracelet in 18K gold and wood with citrine center.

BELOW
Earrings in 18K gold and wood with citrine centers.

Italian creator and designer Roberta Apa Colombo, known simply as Roberta, exudes the warmth of the midday sun and the wisdom of many long winters. She is decidedly a jeweler for the four seasons. Shells and starfish seem gilded in sunlight in her Sea collection, where reflections of the sunrise shimmer with yellow and pink sapphires. The ornate Gipsy collection showcases charms layered with amber and glowing lamps, embellished with turquoise or red coral, each piece alluding to conversations that drift late into the evening. Teakwood, lit with the fires of warm gold topaz and peridot, is the root of the Eco collection, Roberta's autumn line. "I see this for September or November," says Roberta. "When it's raining and chilly, you need a reminder of the summer's warmth. This collection looks great with all white, all beige, and even all black."

For more than twenty years, she has been leading the wave of modern jewelers who create specially for the financially independent women who are increasingly selecting jewelry for themselves. "The same customer

who buys the important pieces for the evening, this is the same woman who is looking for something more comfortable that she can buy for herself, not with the money of the man."

Unfettered individuality is reflected in every jewel, and at the same time, romance, elegance and femininity are intrinsic to each collection. "I understand the life of the woman, because I am a woman. When I create, I create for myself. For me, it's simple," says Roberta. Inspiration abounds for the Italian designer, who began creating jewelry after marrying Luciano Apa, heir to a great tradition of jewelry-making. For hundreds of years, the Apa family designed cameos, and when Roberta joined the company "she brought light into the factory. All colors of the spectrum are in light," says her friend Paolo Peroso. While the family continued to produce its popular cameos, Roberta

ABOVE
Bracelet in 18K gold with lapis lazuli.

ABOVE CENTER
Charm in 18K gold with lapis lazuli.

ABOVE RIGHT
Interior of the boutique.

RIGHT
Bracelet in 18K gold with pink coral, red coral, turquoise and lapis lazuli.

began exploring contemporary design.

Relying far less on platinum and diamonds than many other designers, Roberta crafts jewels in bold colors and contrasting materials, combining crystal and pastel-colored sapphires, teakwood and peridot, and white gold and turquoise. The brilliant blue enhances her striking visage — summer bronzed skin, flowing blonde hair and sparkling green eyes: When Roberta enters a room, it is certain that every head will turn.

Designs for her jewelry are inspired in solitude. "When I am creating, I must be alone. I go to the office on the weekends when no one is there. When I am completely alone on the sand or when I ski, when I am free, my mind can roam."

ABOVE
Ring in 18K white gold with pink sapphires and diamonds.

ABOVE LEFT
Necklaces and earrings in 18K yellow gold and yellow, pink and blue sapphires.

BELOW LEFT
Earrings in 18K white gold with blue sapphires. !8K gold rings with rubies and blue sapphires.

At other times, a personal encounter may spark her creative bent. "Once I met a nice, young girl who wore no jewelry. When I asked her why, she told me she didn't like silver and she couldn't find smaller items that appealed to her," Roberta recalls. "With her in mind, I began creating the Baby collection." Not solely youth-oriented, the collection is a perfect introduction to the world of jewelry

for those who are more comfortable with restrained, refined styles. Pastel sapphires and crystal adorn delicate chains, small hearts and various precious shapes.

Dark moments, too, call forth inspiration. After her husband passed away, Roberta found it difficult to create. Fortunately, she could keep busy with the business of cameo production. She had also begun designing the Gipsy collection — ornate and flamboyant jewelry for bold women — that is now one of her best sellers. "I created the Gipsy collection one year before he died, so I had something from which to draw inspiration."

The first new collection to emerge as she "came back to life" is the Best Wishes line, an exploration of Egyptian symbolism. "I started to think about women and life," she says, pointing to the ancient symbols for success, fertility and love, each adorned and reinvented through her own stylistic spirit.

Each of Roberta's lines is created for different moments in a woman's life, all crafted by the hands of a nurturing soul who is intimate with happiness and sorrow, and who explores the beauty of both through the crafting of jewels.

ABOVE
Cameo brooch in 18K gold, sardonyx shell and diamonds.

ABOVE RIGHT
Red coral necklace in18K gold, pink coral with 18K gold, pink rose earrings and red rose earrings in 18K gold.

RIGHT
Necklace in 18K gold with red coral and jade.

Verdura

THE INTRIGUING STORY OF THE LIFE of the Duke of Verdura is as fascinating as the innovative jewelry he so cleverly designed. The aristocratic Italian duke was internationally known among members of elite society for his chic sense of style and impertinent wit. In the same spirit, Verdura's jewelry creations — while not the most flamboyant or expensive — immediately caught the attention of the rich and famous. Verdura transformed the realm of fine jewelry into a playground for his imagination, without heeding trends or tradition. He replaced platinum with yellow gold and dared to combine brightly colored precious and semiprecious stones, focusing on composition instead of large gems that commonly served as a centerpiece.

LEFT
Gold, purple sapphire, yellow diamond and demantoid garnet flower brooch.

FACING PAGE
Black pearl Lariat necklace with platinum and diamond elements and tassels.

In what reads like a fairy tale, Fulco di Verdura's fascinating life began at the Villa Niscemi outside of Palermo, Sicily, where he was born in 1898. A descendent of Spanish and French kings, Verdura grew up in an idyllic setting: the family estate was verdant with lush gardens that teemed with exotic animals, such as llamas and monkeys. When Verdura's father died, Fulco spent his small inheritance to host a fancy dress ball before leaving Palermo to explore his future.

ABOVE
Platinum and diamond leaves necklace.
LEFT
Gold and diamond woven ring.
FAR LEFT
New Verdura store at 38 Via Mizner, Worth Avenue, Palm Beach, Florida.

Verdura first went to Paris, where he was soon receiving invitations to the most fashionable parties and making important social and business connections. Perhaps the most significant friendship Verdura developed was with Linda and Cole Porter, who led him to Coco Chanel. Chanel and Verdura found common ground in rebellion against traditional fashion, and she helped to launch his career as a designer, first of textiles, then of jewelry. Chanel believed that jewelry boasting expensive stones should be worn together with costume jewelry, and Verdura, sharing that view, began crafting revolutionary items combining multicolored stones. He also created for her personal collection what are now classic pieces, such as a pair of enameled cuff bracelets,

ABOVE
Gold and diamond pine cone brooch.
LEFT
Black onyx, sapphire, ruby, diamond and pearl byzantine cuff bracelet.
FAR LEFT
Fulco di Verdura.

ABOVE
Platinum diamond bow earclips with South Sea pearl drops.

FAR RIGHT
Platinum, diamond and emerald "x" necklace.

BOTTOM
Gold, platinum, diamond and emerald cushion ring.

both bearing a jeweled Maltese cross.

In 1934, Verdura left Chanel to come to America with his close friend, the Russian Baron Nicolas de Gunzburg. Verdura began designing for the prominent jeweler Paul Flato, and was sent to run Flato's store in Hollywood. There, Verdura created jewelry for Hollywood's biggest screen stars, including Marlene Dietrich, Rita Hayworth, Joan Crawford and Katharine Hepburn.

With Cole Porter's help, Verdura opened his own shop in 1939. His reputation grew quickly by word of mouth, and his jewelry soon appeared on the covers of *Harper's Bazaar* and *Vogue* magazines. Possessed by an intense dedication to creating new designs, Verdura spent little effort on self-promotion. He worked in a small office at the rear of his shop on Fifth Avenue and was incredibly productive, making thousands of drawings that are still used today in the development of new pieces.

Verdura was one of the first to incorporate classical motifs such as ropes, coins and caning into popular jewelry. He would turn an Indian chess piece into a brooch by setting it with gems. He collected shells and adorned them with precious stones. Verdura conceived of designs that emulated nature in a way that had not been done since the Renaissance. He created feathers, wings, leaves and animals, which were reminiscent of his childhood in Sicily. He also pioneered the revival of baked enamel.

FAR LEFT
Gold and diamond ray brooch.

LEFT
Yellow gold and brown diamond flower earclips.

BELOW LEFT
Gold and diamond knots necklace.

BELOW
Pair of gold, diamond, turquoise and briolette pink topaz angel brooches.

The clientele of Verdura has always been like a secret association. There has never been a glitzy storefront window, or large marketing campaign. Yet many of the most renowned Americans and Europeans are a part of this elite society. The Duchess of Windsor, known for her love of great jewelry, was one of Verdura's most ardent admirers. So distinct is the Verdura style that demand for his creations grows each time one of his jewels makes a public appearance.

Today, Ward Landrigan, present owner of Verdura, faithfully carries on the jewelrymaker's tradition of quality and cutting-edge style. Landrigan and Executive Vice President Maria Kelleher Williams have reestablished contact with many of Verdura's original jewelers in order to uphold the precise standards established by Verdura himself, ensuring that the tone Verdura set for his exclusive clientele lives on today. Underscoring this tone, as well, is the Verdura salon — discretely located high above Fifth Avenue, with a view of Central Park. The atmosphere is warm and inviting, and a vast selection of Verdura's signature pieces is showcased throughout the spacious salon.

In 1985, when Landrigan bought the jeweler, he inherited more than 4,000 designs

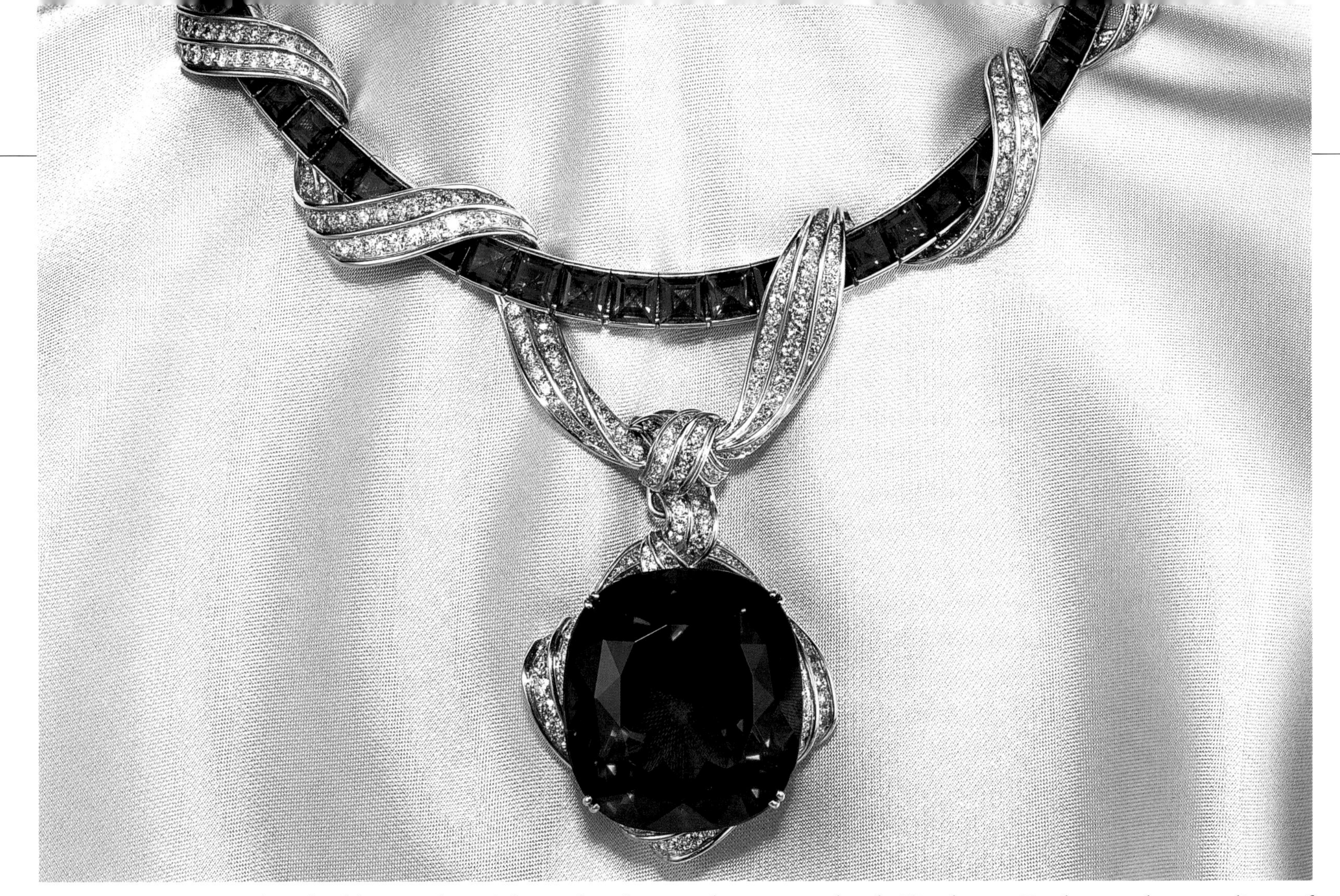

ABOVE
Gold, amethyst and yellow and white diamond ribbon necklace with pendant.

BELOW
Platinum and invisibly set ruby bow brooch.

sketched by Verdura. These sketches are consulted in the creation of new designs that reflect Verdura's style. The jeweler also offers items from Verdura's archives, bought at auction, as stunning and suitable to today's fashions as they were fifty years ago.

Before taking charge of Verdura, Ward Landrigan held the prestigious post of Sotheby's jewelry department chief. He then formed his own estate-jewelry business, where he worked alongside the world's greatest jewelry designers. Throughout his many experiences in the world of jewelry, however, his passion and ultimate goal was always to lead Verdura. Perhaps the quality of Landrigan's that has had the most influence on the company is his understanding that even as fashion changes, eloquent jewelry exists without limitations.

Landrigan has succeeded in retaining the loyal clientele of the past, while attracting a new generation of jewelry connoisseurs. In order to accommodate this growth, a second salon is being opened in Palm Beach: yet another step in the ongoing evolution of the legacy built by Fulco di Verdura. This legacy will continue to thrive, as the rich imagination of Verdura is rediscovered by new generations ready to embrace the artistry that is unmistakably Verdura.

SYNONYMOUS WITH BOLD FASHION, Versace appeals to a vibrant culture yearning to be noticed. A discernable lack of regard for the middle ground coupled with innovations that always surprise are signature elements in Gianni Versace's legacy of epic proportions. Through astonishing versatility, Versace incorporated Baroque and Renaissance motifs, often going to the edge to risk shocking the faint of heart. Versace pursued a clear mission in popularizing the freedom of aesthetic choice—enticing luminaries, celebrities and fashion pundits alike. Such daring extends to all of the many items Gianni Versace has touched, including Versace jewelry, whose striking statement is one that will not be easily forgotten.

ABOVE
Barocco ring. Center stone is a 3-carat, d-flawless diamond, Pavé diamonds total 2.25 carats. Medusas in white gold.

FACING PAGE
Rings from the Barocco, Crocco and Atelier Collections. All center stones are d-flawless diamonds, mounted in white or yellow gold.

Versace

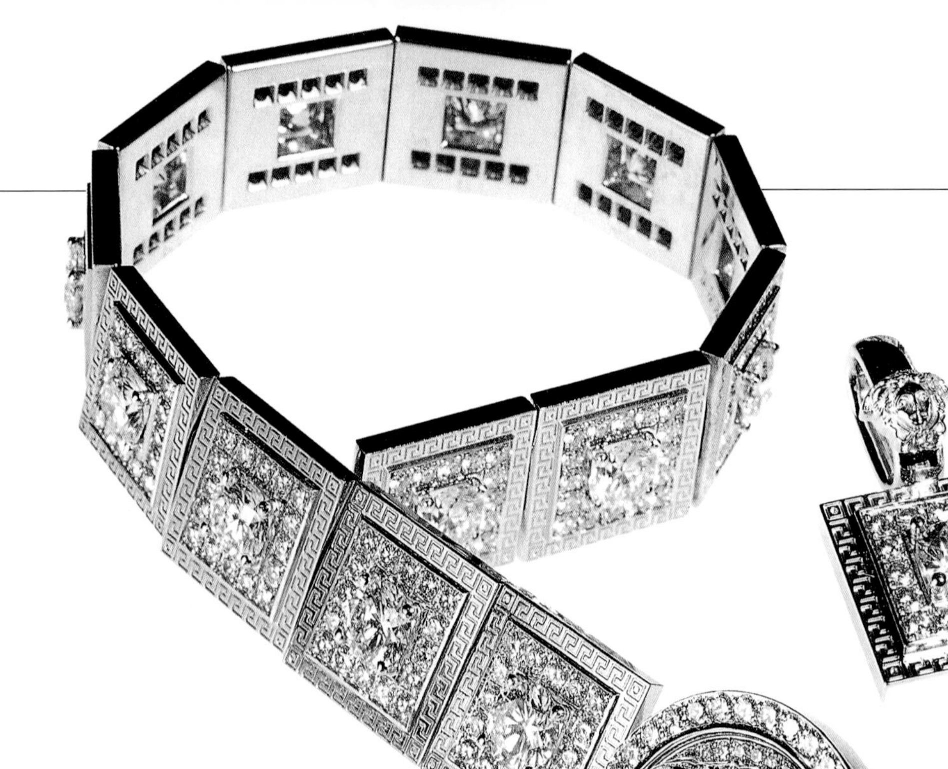

COUNTERCLOCKWISE FROM TOP RIGHT
Atelier Pendant in white gold with a center 1-carat d-flawless stone; Atelier Bracelet in white gold with 12 1-carat d-flawless diamonds; Donatella Versace; Interior of dress shop; The Medusa logo; Sketch of costume design; Black, off-the-shoulder leather gown from the 1997 collections; Barocco ring in white gold with a d-flawless 1-carat center stone. Pavé of 1.60-carat d-flawless diamonds.

The fantasy began in Reggio Calabria, a small southern Italian port city. Here, Gianni Versace was deeply influenced by the city's Greco-Roman past as he was also by his mother's dress shop. With this strong foundation he was able to let his talent and wild imagination flourish into the realization of a lifelong dream. To help him build his empire, Versace engaged the help of his family. His brother Santo became the Chairman and Managing Director of the company. His sister Donatella was given control of Versus, a subisdiary line of clothing embracing youthful fashion. Donatella's own explosive style inspired many of her brother's creations. Needless to say, the emphasis on strong family ties runs throughout the GV Company history.

The premise behind much of what Gianni Versace achieved was his disregard for the barriers between high art and low art. He was both criticized and adored for the blatant sexuality in many of his works. Like other distinct artists, his work roused opinions and debate. Gianni Versace was renowned for daring to combine the styles of the streets with the luxury prized by even those who worshiped him.

Known for his zeal for life, Versace explored every media with vigor. For this reason, Versace's advertising campaigns became nearly as famous as the products themselves. The best photographers were used: Bruce Weber, Richard Avedon and Steven Meisel, to name a few. Under his employ, models became super models.

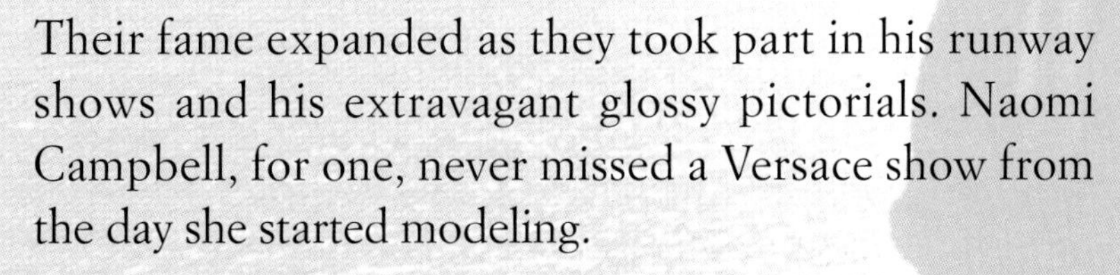

Their fame expanded as they took part in his runway shows and his extravagant glossy pictorials. Naomi Campbell, for one, never missed a Versace show from the day she started modeling.

The rich and famous graced Versace's public and private worlds. Madonna was a friend who also appeared in his advertisements. The rock 'n roll connection included the Artist (Formerly Known as Prince), and Elton John, one of Versace's dearest friends. Versace products have gained great exposure from the many high visibility clients that have worn them. Princess Diana contributed to the cause, as have Elizabeth Hurley and Courtney Love. Love and Hurley reached international stardom partly through their wearing of Versace fashions. Hurley's safety pin dress and Courtney Love's Oscar-night outfit of a GV Atelier Haute-Couture gown are part of fashion history.

ABOVE LEFT
Signature ring in yellow gold with a total weight of 1-carat of d-flawless diamonds.

ABOVE RIGHT
Signature bracelet in yellow gold with Medusas in white gold and d-flawless diamonds weighing 11.5 carats.

RIGHT
Crocco ring in yellow gold, center 1-carat d-flawless daimond, and total pavé of 1.60 d-flawless diamonds.

Pop culture was not the only world that Versace embraced. During the 1980s, he created elaborate costumes for ballet, theater and opera. In 1983, he designed costumes for a Gustav Mahler ballet at the theater of La Scala di Milano, an enterprise that lead him to work with some of the world's most prestigious theaters, such as the San Francisco Opera House, Covent Garden of London and the Opéra Comique of Paris. Versace's brilliance and skill were rewarded with a number of prizes during this period, including "The Cutty Sark," "The Stanley Award" and a valued citation from the Counsel of Fashion Designers of America.

For his contribution in the jewelry industry he was recognized with the 1996 De Beers award for his creation of the stunning and unique Tiara

with 102.04 carats worth of diamonds, each of which is certified d-flawless.

Versace's creations have been exhibited at the Metropolitan Museum of Art and the Museum of Natural History in New York, The Victoria and Albert Museum in London and the Kunst Gewerbemuseum in Berlin. In addition, his work has been celebrated at the Fashion Institute of Technology in New York, the Kobe City Museum in Japan and Villa Stueck in Munich.

Versace was dazzling in his consistency, encompassing his life in art and luxury. He lived as if among the Titans, in Olympian style. Each residence he acquired became more palatial than the last. There was his three-story, 17th-century Palazzo in Milan, and the seventeen-room Villa on Lake Como. His town house on Manhattan's Upper East Side served as a museum for his incredible collection of modern art including Picassos, Lichtensteins and Schnabels. The ultimate in extravagance went to his Miami Beach property, his favorite home and vacation spot.

The Signature style in Versace's clothing line has expanded significantly. A billion-dollar industry has grown to include several fragrances, a line of

ABOVE LEFT
Atelier ring in yellow gold with a center 1-carat d-flawless diamond. Medusas in white gold and pavé of .90-carat d-flawless diamonds.

ABOVE CENTER
Tiara bracelet in yellow gold with Medusa in white gold. Two flowers feature d-flawless center stones weighing 3 carats and d-flawless pavé diamonds totalling 19.8 carats.

CENTER
Tiara necklace in yellow gold. Two flowers feature d-flawless diamonds as center stones weighing 3 carats and d-flawless pavé diamonds totalling 20.5 carats. The clasp flower features a d-flawless, 1-carat diamond at the center.

LEFT
Tiara ring in yellow gold with d-flawless, 3-carat diamond center stone. Pavé diamonds are d-flawless and weigh 5.4 carats.

BELOW
Tiara earrings in yellow gold with d-flawless, 3-carat diamond center stones. Pavé diamonds are d-flawless and weigh 5.47 carats.

home furnishings called "Home Signature," as well as other lines such as Versus, Istante, Istante Classic, Versace Classic, Versace Intimo, Versace Sport, Versace Young, Versace Signature Intimo & Mare, Versace Jeans Couture, Versace Intensive, Versace Accessories, Versace fine jewelry collections and the Versace watch collection in collaboration with Franck Muller.

The Versace jewelry collection is manufactured by the renowned Georg Lauer Jewelry Company, part of the Hammer & Soehne Group, one of Germany's finest jewelry manufactures. Every piece in the collection is hand made from beginning to end, following the strict standards that were set by Gianni Versace himself when the collection was first created in 1990. All of the jewelry is manufactured in 18-karat gold of a slightly rose color. The pieces are adorned with top quality diamonds. The Versace collections are always produced in numbered editions, each piece is engraved with the Versace emblem and the edition number. A certificate of identification also presented with each piece of jewelry.

The world of Versace jewelry is a thrilling one, replete with flamboyant sex appeal and fabulous opulence. His heartfelt salute to contemporary art and the great masters of the early twentieth century demonstrates the profound influence of art on Versace's visionary style, a legacy that flourishes and lives on through his sister Donatella, the new chief designer and creative force of today.

CENTER
Signature rings in yellow or white gold with a a total weight of 1.56 d-flawless diamonds. Top left ring has cabochon rubies with black enamal while the top right ring has cabochon saphires.

LOWER LEFT
Signature earrings in yellow gold black enamal and 1.40 carats of d-flawless diamonds.

LOWER RIGHT
Signature tie pin in yellow gold.

Photo Credits

front cover: Chopard. flap: de Grisogono. back cover: de Grisogono for Chopard. back flap: Verdura. p1: Boucheron. p2: Roberta. p3: Piranesi. p4: Chaumet. p5: Martin Gruber. p6-7: Piranesi. p9: Alexandre Reza. p11: Boucheron. p12: Chopard. P15: Verdura. p16: Versace. p18: Alexandre Reza. p20: Alexandre Reza. p21: The Louvre. p22: National Archeological Museum of Athens; The Royal Palace Museum, Naples; Boucheron; Chaumet. p23: The Cairo Museum; Chaumet; Eugene Delacroix. p24: The Louvre; The Troyes Museum; Musée Toulouse-Lautrec; Nigerian Museum, Lagos; p25: Musée Barbier-Mueller; National Archeological Museum of Athens; New York Library; The Louvre; Sygma/Tim Graham; Boucheron; Lalaounis; Van Cleef & Arpels. p26: Bibliotecca Nazionale Central, Firenze; Van Cleef & Arpels; Chaumet. p27: Chaumet; New Delhi National Museum; Sygma. p28: The Louvre; Versailles; Chaumet. p29: The Louvre, Versailles. p30: Chaumet; Maxim's de Paris; Versailles; Alphonse Mucha. p31: Chanel; Boucheron; Chaumet; Petit Palais. p32: Chaumet; Van Cleef & Arpels. p33: Boucheron; Van Cleef & Arpels. p34: Van Cleef & Arpels; Piranesi. p35: Versace. p36: Chaumet. p37: Eugene Delacroix. p38: Eugene Delacroix; Saint-Raymond Museum of Toulouse; Nairobi Museum; Metropolitan Museum of New York; Cairo Museum; Boucheron. p39: National Archeological Museum of Athens; Lalaounis; Boucheron; Saint Germain Museum; Musée Chatillon-sur-Seine; National Archeological Museum of Athens. p40: New Delhi National Museum; Victoria and Albert Museum. p41: Van Cleef & Arpels; New Delhi National Museum. p42: The Louvre; Versailles; Alexandre Dumas; Versailles. p43: Van Cleef & Arpels; Chaumet. p44: Leon Benouville; Van Cleef & Arpels. p45: Piranesi; Boucheron; Alexandre Reza; Mauboussin. p46: Alexandre Reza; Piranesi; Van Cleef & Arpels. p47: Van Cleef & Arpels. p48: Chopard; Boucheron; Christian Coigny. p49: Piranesi; Boucheron; Van Cleef & Arpels. p50: Piranesi; Alexandre Reza; Boucheron. p51: Boucheron. p52: Alexandria Museum, Egypt; Museum of Cairo. p53: Palace of Artaxerxes. p54: Musée de Beaux Arts; Vatican Museum; Palmyra Museum; Lalaounis. p55: MusÈe de Grenoble; National Palace Museum of Taipei. p56: British Airways; Madras Museum of India; Musée de l'Homme; The Louvre. p57: The Louvre; Versailles; Eugene Delacroix; Bulgari; Lalaounis. p58: Alexandre Reza; Versace; Piranesi; p59: Van Cleef & Arpels. p60: Alexandre Reza. p61: Van Cleef & Arpels. p62: Chaumet; National Archeological Museum of Athens; Petit Palais. p63: Lalaounis; Michelangelo; Vatican Museum; Troyes Museum; Chaumet. p64: Piranesi; Chaumet; Alexandre Reza; Boucheron. p65: Chanel; Boucheron; de Grisogono; Alexandre Reza. p66: New Delhi National Museum; Boucheron; de Grisogono; Alexandre Reza; New Delhi National Museum; Boucheron; Chaumet. p67: Van Cleef & Arpels; Chaumet; Van Cleef & Arpels. p68: Boucheron. p69: Chaumet; Alexandre Reza; Boucheron. p70: Mauboussin; Van Cleef & Arpels; Boucheron. p71: Boucheron; Versace. p72: Mauboussin; Van Cleef & Arpels, Boucheron. p73: Henri Matisse; Chanel. p74: Vienna Museum. p75: Eugene Delacroix. p76: Eugene Delacroix; Musée de l'Homme, Paris; Madras Museum, India. p77: Cairo Museum; Dakar Museum; The Louvre, Paris. p78: The Egyptian Museum; Museum Saint-Germain; Lalaounis; Boucheron archives; Van Cleef & Arpels. p79: Pushkin Museum; Musée Saint-Germain; Vienna Museum; Boucheron; Musée Saint-Germain. p80: Archaeological Museum of Athens; Doris Panos; Lalaounis. p81: Lalaounis; Doris Panos. p82: New Delhi Museum, India; Archaeological Museum, Chatillon-sur-Seine; Alexandre Reza. p83: New Delhi National Museum; Alexandre Reza. p84: Alphonse Mucha; Le Petit-Palais; Piranesi. p85: Mauboussin; Chaumet; Cartier. p86: Mauboussin; Van Cleef & Arpels; Alexandre Reza; Boucheron. p87: Chaumet. p88: Dakar Museum. p89: Musée Barbier-Mueller. p90: Grand Palais, Paris; Royal Museum of Central Africa; New Delhi National Museum. p91: Cairo Museum; courtesy of Egypt Air; Nigerian Museum. p92: New Delhi National Museum; Cairo Museum; Auxere Musée des Beaux Art; Lalaounis. p93: New Delhi National Museum. p94: The Louvre; Boucheron; Versailles. p95: New Delhi National Museum; Versailles; La Mal Maison. p96: Gustav Klimt; Maxim's de Paris; Martin Gruber; Mauboussin. p97: Mauboussin; Boucheron. p98: Boucheron; Alexandre Reza; Chopard. p99: Versace; de Grisogono; Alexandre Reza; Chaumet; Boucheron; Chanel; Piranesi; Chopard; Piranesi. p100: Chanel; Versace; Boucheron; Verdura; Chaumet. p102: Druout, Paris. p103: Versailles. p104: National Palace Museum of Taipei; Boucheron. p105: Boucheron; Chaumet. p106: Boucheron; de Grisogono; Iribf. p107: Mauboussin; Samaritan Store, Paris; Druout, Paris; Chaumet; Verdura. p108: Chaumet; Boucheron; Lalaounis; Chaumet; Boucheron; Chaumet. p109: Verdura; Versace; de Grisogono. p111-119: Alexandre Reza. p120-127: Boucheron. p128-135: Chanel. p130: V.H. Grandpierre ©All rights reserved. D.R. p136-143: Chaumet. p144-151: Chopard. p152-157: Roberto Coin. p158-163: de Grisogono. p164-169: Martin Gruber. p170-175: Lalaounis. p176-181: Doris Panos. p182-189: Piranesi. p190-195: Roberta. p196-201: Verdura. p202-207: Versace.

FACING PAGE
Gold, diamond, pearl, ruby, emerald and sapphire rhino brooch. Verdura.

Bibliography

ART NOUVEAU: JEWELS AND JEWELERS
Elise B. Misiorowski and Dona M. Dirlam
Gems & Gemology, Winter 1986
Gemological Institute of America

THE BOOK OF THE PEARL
George Krenz and Charles Stevenson
1908

BOUCHERON
Gilles Neret
Rizzoli

CHAUMET: MASTER JEWELERS SINCE 1980
Alain de Gourcoff
Chaumet, 1995

CHAUMET: TWO CENTURIES OF FINE JEWELRY
Musée Carnavalet

THE COMPLETE TUTANKHAMUN
Nicholas Reeves
Thames and Hudson, 1990

DREAMS OF YESTERDAY, REALITIES OF TODAY
Alexandre Reza
Arlette SETA
Editions d'Art Monelle, 1991

ENGAGEMENT AND WEDDING RINGS
A. Matlins, A. Bonanno and J. Crystal
Gemstone Press

EXTRAORDINARY JEWELS
John Traina
Doubleday, 1991

GEMS & GEMOLOGY
Vol. 25, No. 2, pp. 68-83
Gemological Institute of America, 1989

GOLD OF AFRICA
Timothy F. Garrad
Barbier Mueller

HOLLYWOOD JEWELS: aMOVIES, JEWELRY,STARS
Penny Proddow
Harry N. Abrams

JEWELRY BY CHANEL
Patrick Mauries
Bulfinch, 1993

MAUBOUSSIN
Marguerite de Cerval
Editions du Regard, 1992

MAXIM'S DE PARIS
Marianne Rufenacht
Jour Azur, 1982

METAMORPHOSES
Ilias Lalounis
1984

OBJECTS OF ADORNMENT 5000 YEARS OF JEWELRY
Walters Art Gallery, Baltimore

ROIS ET REINES DE FRANCE
Jean Raspail and Elisabeth Kirchhhoff
Edition A Images, 1997

SECRET OF THE HAREM
Carla Coco
The Vendôme Press, 1997

THE STORY OF JEWELRY
J. Anderson Black
William Morrow & Co., 1974

VAN CLEEF & ARPELS
Sylvie Raulet
Edition du Regard, 1986

VERSAILLES
Edition A Images

FACING PAGE
Sapphire ring adorned with baguette-cut diamonds and round-cut diamonds in 18K yellow gold. Boucheron.